NEYMAR
MY STORY
CONVERSATIONS WITH MY FATHER

NEYMAR JR AND NEYMAR SR

WITH IVAN MORÉ

TRANSLATED BY FELIPE DE CARVALHO

First published in Great Britain in 2014 by
ARENA SPORT
An imprint of Birlinn Limited
West Newington House
10 Newington Road
Edinburgh
EH9 1QS

www.arenasportbooks.co.uk

ISBN: 978-1-909715-26-4
eBook ISBN: 978-0-85790-830-8

First published in Brazil in 2013 by
Universo dos Livros Editora Ltda. as
Neymar: Conversa entre pai e filho

British Library Cataloguing-in-Publication Data
A catalogue record for this book is available on request from the
British Library.

Designed and typeset by Polaris Publishing, Edinburgh

Printed by Clays St Ives Plc

CONTENTS

FOREWORD

ACOLD WEEKDAY AFTERNOON in Wroclaw, Poland, was made much less ordinary by the presence of the Brazilian national football team, who were in town for a friendly against Japan. It was October 2012 and the first time in over a year that Kaka, the last Brazilian player to win the Ballon d'Or, had played for the Seleção (the moniker for the national team in Brazil). There were so many reasons for everybody, from journalists to autograph hunters, to keep their attention fixed firmly on that training session, which is why it is so remarkable that every spectator's head turned towards the stands when a trim, middle-aged man emerged from the tunnel. Neutral observers would be excused if they thought the man suddenly surrounded by cameras and microphones was a former Brazil player.

But Neymar Sr's footballing career never reached those heights. Instead, it is his role in bringing up his only son, named after him, that has made the man famous in Brazil. While the world of sport is full of stories of athletes' parents becoming celebrities, Neymar Sr stood out for seeking to do the exact opposite, though he has never hidden his pride in helping his son become Brazilian football's great new hope.

Anybody with even a minimal interest in the game these days knows about Neymar Jr's exploits. In the last four years he has become the reference point for the Seleção: top goal scorer, the poster boy for Nike's advertising campaigns, and the main threat obsessed about by opposition managers and players. What few people are aware of, however, is how instrumental his father's guidance has been to his meteoric rise. And while Neymar Sr knew that his son's success could change the lives of a family struggling to make ends meet, he never put pressure on him, nor did he lose sight of the importance of forming the young man's character as well as developing his footballing skills.

When Neymar Jr was born, in February 1992, things were not going well for the family. Struggling to put food on the table, Neymar Sr was forced to move his wife, son and daughter, Rafaela, to a room at his parents' house in São Vicente, a seaside town near Santos in the south of São Paulo state. With money extremely tight, one of the few luxuries the family could afford was the fee to join Tumiaru, a local and humble social club where Neymar Jr would spend hours kicking a ball.

When Neymar Jr was ten, he was offered a place at the youth academy at local club Portuguesa Santista. While many parents would have simply seized the opportunity for a cash injection, Neymar Sr realised that he had a chance to improve his children's lives on another level. Thanks to contacts in the club, both Neymar Jr and Rafaela were awarded scholarships at one of the most prestigious private schools in Santos.

At the beginning of the 90s, one in five Brazilians over the age of 15 was illiterate, and studies conducted by the Brazilian Football Confederation showed that the bulk of professional players in Brazil had left school without any decent qualifications. What is even more striking is that statistics also showed that the majority of footballers in Brazil earned less than €1000 a month. Neymar Sr feared that his son might not make it as a professional player, so he was insistent that he worked hard on his education. As time would tell, Neymar Sr's fears, although both wise and admirable, would prove unwarranted. Emerging at a time when clubs in

Brazil and abroad were stepping up their pursuit of younger and younger talents to sign to their academies, Neymar Jr's talents were quickly recognised and offers started to roll in for more money than the family had ever seen. That was when Neymar Sr excelled again. First, he had the courage of his convictions to turn down a lucrative approach from Real Madrid when his son was 13, choosing instead to bet on Santos FC's long-established track record in player development. Then, he had the presence of mind not to spoil his son with luxuries despite the years of hardship they had endured.

As well as establishing limits on how much Neymar could spend every month, his father made a rule that treats could only be earned through performances on the pitch. To get his first car, for example, Neymar had to win the under-20 South American Championship with the Seleção in 2010. Even his earrings were the result of a bet with his father.

These tales are just a taste of what you will find in this book. Different from a great number of footballer's biographies, this one focuses on a dialogue between a father and son. In several ways these two are inseparable and this book goes to great lengths to explain a relationship that has become a rarity in modern times, not just in the sports world.

Here, you will find stories of triumph and despair, some that were unknown even to Brazilians prior to the publication of this book – such as the car accident that almost claimed an infant Neymar Jr's life. Most of all it sheds light on the genesis of a player whose success serves as model for younger players around the world. In a country where football still stands as an important way to escape the poverty trap, both Neymars have valuable lessons to teach.

Through this book you will come to understand that Neymar Jr might never have reached his current status without the care, attention and work of his father. The most interesting aspect of this relationship is that Neymar Jr has never tried to downplay the influence of his father. Where many other potentially outstanding Brazilian players have faltered and slipped into obscurity, Neymar Jr's family have proved to be a crucial source of support and one that the superstar footballer has never forgotten.

Even for people who are very familiar with Brazilian football, this book brings new insight into the transformation of a hopeful young boy into a global superstar. Still in his early twenties, Neymar Jr has just started his life in European football and most of his accolades have been won in Brazil. Important names around the world have fallen over themselves to sing his praises and predict great things for his career. Statistics alone will not explain to you why.

So enjoy reading as father and son open their hearts. As somebody who has met both of them on several occasions, I cannot recommend enough that you pay attention to what these two have to say.

Fernando Duarte, London, May 2014

INTRODUCTION

I FIRST MET NEYMAR Jr on 11 April 2009, shortly after he had made his professional debut for Santos FC, one of Brazil's grand old football institutions and the club where Pelé had made his name. I remember that day so clearly. Santos were playing one of their great rivals, Palmeiras, in the Campeonato Paulista semi-final first leg at Santos' magnificent home ground, Vila Belmiro. Neymar Jr scored the winning goal, with his left foot, as the home team recorded a 2-1 victory.

He was replaced late in the second half and, after clearing permission from Vanderlei Luxemburgo, the Santos coach, I went to the bench, sat beside Neymar Jr and asked if he could take off his left boot. I wanted to take a photo of it to accompany my match report. I remember the look on his young face – surprised and slightly bemused by the strange request. Nevertheless, he smiled and handed me his boot.

Thus began my friendly but respectful relationship with Neymar Jr. During his early days in the Santos jersey, I had the chance to write some exclusive reports on him and I could see just what a special player he was, even at seventeen. As his star has risen to stratospheric heights, there has been a steady and constant influence over his life and career, someone who has been by his side every step of the way: his father, Neymar Sr.

Neymar Jr, and all those that know him well or who have any in-depth knowledge of his career, know he would not have become the player that he is without his father. And only when one understands his father's past does one come to fully understand the challenges that the Neymar family have faced and overcome. Only then can one truly understand the making of this extraordinary footballer.

The purpose of this book is to show how Neymar Jr's success came to be. How did this young man emerge from an impoverished background to become the greatest name in modern-day Brazilian sport? What ignited his passion for the game and how was it nurtured? How did he develop his wondrous skills and relentless work ethic? How did he harness his passion for the game and channel it so that he could be the best he could be, and develop the belief that he could make it to the very top of world football?

There are only two people who are able to truly answer these questions: Neymar Sr and Neymar Jr. The story of the role and the influence that each has had on the other's life, and how they have achieved such a successful balance between work and family life, is both beautiful and touching. And so this book is told by them, in their own words, as it should be.

Neymar Jr's talent has always been something quite extraordinary. But it could have been lost to the football world had it not been carefully nurtured, developed and managed.

This story reveals the making of one of the greatest, and most iconic, players on the planet.

Ivan Moré, Brazil, 2013

FROM FATHER TO SON

MY NAME IS NEYMAR da Silva Santos. Neymar is not a very common name, but I guess it has become increasingly recognised because of a very special person who came into my life on 5 February 1992. Silva and Santos are very common surnames in Brazil. There are Silvas everywhere. Even presidents have been named Silva. And Santos is another name of which I am very proud. I'm proud of my son, who built for himself a wonderful chapter in the history of Santos Futebol Clube, the team of my idol, Pelé, and of many other great players who have emerged from Vila Belmiro, the club's historic home ground. Santos is the team that is the nearest to my heart and it is the team that has helped shape my son's career.

But nobody in our family was more fanatical about Santos FC than my father, Seu Ilzemar. He and my mother were from Espírito Santo in south-eastern Brazil, and while my brothers, José Benício (whom everyone calls Nicinho) and Jane (who we call Joana D'Arc), and I were all born in Santos, there is no doubt that my father wished that we had all been born within the Vila Belmiro stadium itself!

Unfortunately, Seu Ilzemar didn't see his grandson playing professionally – he died in May 2008, less than a year before Neymar Jr's debut for Santos FC. But my son inherited his grandfather's respect and admiration for the club and whenever he played I know that he took the memory and love of his grandfather onto the pitch with him.

For Neymar Jr, or Juninho, as we call him in the family, his career has been like a carnival. This does not mean that he plays with thoughtless abandon or with a reckless disregard for his privileged position, but that he has enjoyed a complete and unbridled joy in his career. Everything he ever wanted in life, he has in his job. All he needs to be happy is a field, a goal and a ball. But nothing came easy for him – or for us. We had to overcome many adversities to get where we are today. Nothing was ever handed to him; even with his talents, he has had to earn his way to the top. The secret to this has been simple: dedication. He has shown endless dedication to work on his game and develop his skills, and those of us who love him most and who have believed in him from the beginning have shown our dedication to his dreams through our own sacrifice and investment. And it is wonderful to be able to look back now, even at this stage of his career, and know that it has all has been worth it.

Every professional athlete lives in a world that often seems unreal. There are many hurdles on the journey to professional level, and it is even harder to push onto the next level to become a superstar. And the thing is, when an athlete retires, he can't simply change jobs. He needs to find a completely different career. And that is a very hard thing to do.

It is a cruel irony that when a footballer is at his finest, both as an athlete and as a man, when he feels mature and responsible, the body starts to feel the toll of so much effort and sacrifice. It's possible to sidestep past your adversaries, but you can't sidestep past time. Time comes to everyone. And a competitor, by definition, always wants to win. But, in this fight, you can't win. You need to know the best time to quit. But who can really tell when that is?

I, for instance, was also a professional footballer. I too started at the Santos youth academy. From the ages of 14 to 16 I represented my beloved team, then I went to Portuguesa Santista to become a professional player. From there I went to Tanabi, in São Paulo, when I was still very young. After that, I played for a team in the third division of the state of Minas Gerais called Iturama, near Frutal, where I caught tuberculosis. I had to rest for an entire year and did not play again until I was 20.

There was no way I could play professionally under those circumstances. My game, my fitness, my strength and my stamina had all suffered. I had decided to go back to work with my father in his garage when I received an invitation to play for Jabaquara, an established team based in Santos with a rich football history, and which had been a major club until the 1960s.

My father didn't want me to return to football. I was doing all right, earning decent money selling used cars. I repaired the cars at the garage and made a respectable profit when selling them on. My father didn't want me to give up that job security to try my luck again as a footballer. But I did it anyway. I loved to play and I couldn't turn my back on the opportunity. I worked during weekdays with cars and at the weekends I played for

Jabaquara. My love for football was so strong that I was playing without getting paid.

I played four good matches for the Jabuca. One of them was against União FC from Mogi das Cruzes, who were then in the third division of the Campeonato Paulista (the São Paulo state league). Jabaquara was in the fourth division. It was a great opportunity for me to show my value. I did well in that game – so well that the referee, the famous Dulcídio Wanderley Boschilia, advised the managers of União to hire me.

And, what do you know, they accepted the suggestion! My father didn't like that I was playing for Jabaquara – in his head, it wasn't a real job (which was fair enough as I wasn't being paid). However, with União FC, it was more of a professional deal.

When I arrived in Mogi das Cruzes the club management sent me straight into action with the other players, who were training in the city of Suzano, near the capital. I did very well at that first training session, playing as a right winger. I dribbled and carried the ball effectively, and linked up well with the other players. I played exactly as I had at Jabaquara and, I must say, I was very good in my debut under the circumstances.

After the training session, I went to Mogi das Cruzes to sign the contract with the club president. Since I hadn't been paid by Jabaquara, any money from União FC was good. This all happened in March 1989. They offered me a one-year contract. It was a good amount of money, way above my expectations. I tried not to show my enthusiasm, but I was dying to close the deal right there. But I knew how to negotiate and when they laid out the terms of the deal I told them that I had to think about it and would come back to them with my answer at a later date. It was a gamble because I had no idea how much they really wanted me on their books. When I went back for the second meeting I was incredibly nervous, but I tried to keep my cool. The president sat down and slid a revised contract across the table to me. When I read through it I could barely believe my eyes – he had almost doubled the offer. It was hard to maintain a poker face, but I think I managed it and left the office with the deal closed.

I learned a lot in that meeting. And I played very well that year, in the third division. So much so that second division club Rio Branco began to show an interest in me. In December 1989, ten entrepreneurs from Mogi das Cruzes clubbed together to buy my rights and then offered them to União FC, to ensure that I couldn't be poached by another club. With my share of the deal, I bought a little house for my parents in Santos. It was the first time I felt like a rich man – even though it really wasn't like that. I felt rich because I was able to repay my parents for all they had done for me and my brothers. And there's no better feeling in this world.

My deal with União FC stipulated that I would play for them in the first semester of the season (the Brazilian season is divided into two semesters, with regional tournaments in the first, national championships in the second), and then I would play for other clubs on loan, since the team didn't have any professional activities for the rest of the year. That way I played for Coritiba, Lemense and Catanduvense, returning to União FC shortly afterwards.

I have no shame in admitting that I wasn't the best player around, but I wasn't a bad player either. I knew what to do with the ball and had a good vision of the game. But we can't always do what we imagine. The body often doesn't keep up with the mind. Only the very best players can see everything and still execute their vision. That is what sets the elite apart from the rest.

In my case, I suffered injuries that forced me to end my career when I was 32 years old. I had to stop playing professionally too early. I had to give up my passion, my work. I also suffered with bad contracts and bad conditions at various clubs. And I wasn't a kid anymore; I had increasing responsibilities as a family man. Juninho was born in 1992 and on 11 March 1996, my daughter, Rafaela, was born. With her and Juninho to raise, it became difficult to travel to different cities trying to close deals that weren't, ultimately, enough to make ends meet.

Furthermore, taking my son from school to school was too stressful for us and horrible for him. We just couldn't do it anymore, and my body was starting to suffer, too. When I managed to train hard during the week, by the time the match came around all my muscles would hurt. If I spared myself in training, my technique and strategy would suffer during the game. The managers started to suspect I had become lazy, but that wasn't the case at all. The truth is that, physically, I just couldn't take it anymore. The contracts paid less and less and because of my injury record, I was only offered contracts that could be terminated immediately if I suffered another injury.

I felt a lot of pain. I had to treat myself at home so the managers wouldn't know about my problems. I couldn't lie to myself and my employers anymore. I had to choose, which is always hard when you do something you love so much, which you feel is part of your very make-up. Football can do that to you – it gets into your soul. To end your childhood dreams, even when you're an adult and have a family, is always a tough choice. But there was no other way. I had to give up my dream and accept that my career as an athlete was finally over.

However, at that time, I was comforted by two precious jewels at home. One of whom would surpass all my dreams.

FROM SON TO FATHER

WHAT I AM, WHAT I have, I owe to my parents and to God. I'm extremely lucky that I have more than just a father; I have by my side, more than anything else, my best friend. He sometimes is harsh with me, but everything he does, he does it for me, for us. For our family. Fathers are everything to their sons, and that's no different with me. My father is always thinking of what is best for us all and I have learnt so much from his wise advice over the years. He has been my mentor both in football and in life. We all make mistakes and as we are growing up these mistakes are often made because of our inexperience. My father has always helped me to see my mistakes, to avoid them whenever possible, but also to learn from them when they occur. Football has been a tool for shaping who I am as a person: it has helped me evolve my personality by understanding the importance of discipline, teamwork, of placing yourself within the context of a team environment, knowing that you can only truly thrive if you work hard with and for others. No one can ever stand alone – in life or in football – and greatness can only be achieved through dedication and hard work. If my father has taught me anything, it is that.

My father is so much more than a manager, an agent or an advisor. His love and support have been central to all my achievements. I know that I still have a lot to learn, that in many ways I'm still a kid. But I know I can always count on my dad as a reference, on and off the field. I've always looked up to everything he does and says. So many times on the pitch (and in life), I have thought, 'What would my father do in a situation like this?' This always helped me. He is my inspiration.

When I am on the pitch, I also get inspired by other great athletes and idols. My father taught me to always pay attention and learn from more experienced people. So, I always keep an eye on Lionel Messi, Cristiano Ronaldo, and I have always tried to learn something from Ronaldo, Robinho, Romário and Rivaldo.

I realise that I am a public figure. That's why I have to be careful with what I do on and off the field. I know that I'm a role model for many children. I need to be responsible – but it is easier when you love what you do.

I do things my way. It's not an act, I don't like to make up stories. It's not a publicity stunt either. I like being authentic. I love working on my appearance, making bold choices for clothes, shoes, hats and earrings, but I think that's just part of my generation; I don't see anything wrong with that. My hair might change from time to time, but my feet are always firmly on the ground. This is me.

I deal with criticism calmly. I don't feel anger. I know I still have a lot to learn and I know I need to improve. But I also know when criticism is constructive or when things are being exaggerated to sell stories or to create a narrative for television. Fortunately, I feel that I am able to separate these two scenarios, although sometimes the critics don't feel like doing the same. It takes patience and also persistence to get better and try to make those who criticise today speak well of you in the next game.

I'm used to criticism because I have an honest friend in my house. I come home and say, 'What's up, Dad?' and Neymar Sr doesn't show mercy. 'Son, you made a mistake there, and also there! But you can improve from it.' And that's how we learn, right? The key to everything is communication. Empty criticism is no good; but with constructive criticism you can make a real difference.

Like my father, I don't like losing. I have inherited his competitive instinct and I will do all I can in any given match to drive my team to victory. I've always tried to give my best, to bring joy to the fans. I take the responsibility and I never hide from it. I want the ball. I want to play. I don't like when I miss in front of goal and I hate wasting a good pass. I am hard on myself, I really am. But that's how you learn. I want to be the same on the field as when I used to play in the streets: to play with the same spirit and boldness and joy; to never be afraid.

My dad is the best critic I have. The best and the harshest. After the games, we sit down and analyse all my plays and he gives me a copy so I can go away, work and improve. He shows statistics, he tells me what I did wrong, where I was right and how to get better. He knows a lot. It's a truly valuable football lesson. That's how I learn. And I'm very thankful to him for everything.

BARELY MADE IT

EBRUARY, 1992. WE WERE at home when Nadine's waters broke. We went to the maternity ward and, thank God, everything went smoothly. It was a natural birth. And it was a boy! We didn't know until then as we had had no money at the time for an ultrasound.

When our first child was born, we struggled to find a name. The best contender was Mateus, which was Nadine's suggestion. But we couldn't decide. Almost a week passed without a decision. Juninho (his family nickname) lived his first week on Earth without a name. To this day still I'm kind of like that. I take my time deciding certain things. I do everything at the last minute. But when I decide, I never go back. So, when I went to register his name, we had settled on Mateus. However, halfway there I changed my mind, and we named him Neymar. Like his father. And so Neymar Jr came to be.

At the time, Nadine and I lived in an apartment rented by

União FC in Rodeio in Santa Catarina in the south of Brazil. It was there that Neymar Jr spent his first days; I was terrified to hold him in my arms, I had no idea how to take care of such a fragile little thing. In the beginning, I needed someone to help me hold him. Of course, after a while, I learned how to take good care of him. I even started to feel jealous if someone else spent too much time with him.

In June 1992, we went to Santos to visit some relatives. I had played for União FC earlier that day. Juninho was only four months old. I was driving with Nadine at my side, and our son was sleeping soundly, strapped into the baby seat in the back of the car. Driving down the mountain on a rainy day is always dangerous, especially on a road with a single lane and two-way traffic. A car came in our direction. I swerved to the left. I was in fifth gear at the time and the swerve was slow and laboured. When I pressed the accelerator, I was still too slow and there was no time to downshift to gain speed. The other car crashed into us and went through my door. My left leg ended up above my right leg. My pubis, my pelvis – all were dislodged in my body. I was in shock and then the pain hit and I started to yell to my wife, 'I'm dying, I'm dying!' It all happened so fast and amid the shock and pain everything was confused. And then there dawned a thought that was even worse than the pain: where was Juninho? Where was my son?

Nadine was in a great deal of pain as well but we both forced ourselves around to check on him in the back – and we were horrified to see that he had vanished. He was not in the front, nor in the back. Had he been thrown from the car? That's all I could think. That little thing of only four months old . . . I don't think I will ever have the words to describe the feelings that we endured in those dreadful moments. I shudder just to remember. We were almost certain we had lost our son. In the middle of the despair and with the pain, I can only remember praying to God to take me instead of my son. If I had lost him, it would have been unbearable. Incomparable to the pain I felt in the middle of that smashed car.

The car had stopped on the edge of a cliff. There was a stream nearby and we were hanging just above it. Nadine couldn't get out through her door, or else she would fall off the cliff edge. She had to climb out through the back window. I was still trapped by the seatbelt and the crumpled side of the car. After the crash, everything was collapsing around us. Juninho was missing. We were desperate.

Then we heard voices as people rushed to help us. They pulled open the back passenger door and, thank God, they found Juninho under the back seat. The impact of the crash had ripped him from his seat and he had fallen into the foot well and out of sight. When they took him out, he was covered in blood and was taken immediately to hospital. I only saw my wife and son much later; he had been cleaned up and had a bandage over his head – all that blood had come from a small cut in his head made by a shard of glass. Nothing serious had happened, which was a miracle.

I had suffered a very serious dislocation of my pelvis. Since you can't immobilise the area with a plaster cast, the doctors made a special belt which suspended my body in the air. I hung suspended like that in hospital for ten days before being transferred home – where I spent a further four months the same way, lying prone while my body slowly healed.

It wasn't until eight months after the accident that I was able to hold Juninho in my arms again. He was a one-year-old by then and had finally managed to stop crying every time he saw me. In the beginning, he was frightened to see all that equipment holding me in the air. That was terrible for him. And for me, there was an incredible sadness at not having my son around. It was very strange not being able to touch him, to get close to him, or to help my wife to take care of him.

I could only get some sleep late at night, after Juninho and Nadine were already sleeping. I would cry myself to sleep. It was horrible not being able to sit or to move. It was terrifying to think about my future as an athlete after something like that.

But maybe all those trials and all that pain prepared me for the future. I am thankful for the accident. I have more faith and patience now. I have a perspective on life that I didn't have before. It's better to suffer yourself than to see your children suffering. I don't think I could coped if something like that had happened to one of my children.

The greatest pride and satisfaction that I feel is in seeing everything going well for Neymar Jr and Rafaela. If I could do it all over again, I wouldn't change a thing in my life.

FIRST MATCHES

IT WAS MY FATHER who introduced me to the ball. I clearly remember the day, when I was at the stadium watching one of his matches, that I truly started to play football, instead of running after the ball like it was just another toy.

My father was out on the field, playing for real while I was running in the stadium seats and watching the match. I was just playing around, running around more than my father was on the field. I ran up and down the stairs between the seats, never stopping. And the funniest thing about that day was that I wasn't actually kicking a ball: I was running more than playing football. And then, Betinho showed up.

Betinho was a coach from Santos, a very experienced guy. He sat and watched the game, but became distracted by the small figure racing around in the stand beside him. He watched me for a while and was intrigued by the way I was running. He said he saw something in it: a balance, an inherent athleticism. And he began to wonder if I could become a good player. Or at least if I was worth a shot.

Betinho talked to my parents and asked my father if he could start to train me. That was the start, where it all began. It was great to have Betinho take me under his wing. There is no doubt that both he and my father helped me become who I am today. How many talents out there are wasted because of a lack of direction? We all know stories of someone with potential who didn't make it because there was no one to put him on the right path. I was lucky; I know that. And I will never forget it. Without their guidance I could have been just like thousands of other children who show potential but are ultimately lost to the game.

I was fortunate to have a mentor like my father right there, at home, analysing my game, watching over me, guiding me; and then I had a teacher like Betinho, who saw my potential, worked to exploit my virtues, and corrected my weaknesses. Being humble and listening to those who know more and who have lived more is fundamental to learning. Life experience is so important and should never be dismissed.

But improvisation is also essential in football, and I learned to do this very early in life, playing futsal. (Futsal is an indoor version of football and is played with a heavier ball; it is an important part of Brazilian football culture and many experts believe that it has helped develop the dribbling and passing skills for which Brazilian players are traditionally famed.) You might have some play in mind and train that a lot. However, it is only in the heat of the game that you'll discover whether it works or not. In those moments, you need to really feel the game, to sense the play and whether it is the right moment to try something special. A lot of the things that I did on the indoor pitch, and even on the grass fields, were made on the fly, based solely on instinct. The secret is that it's possible to 'train' how to improvise and to play with that kind of creative instinct. How many times did I do that at home? I used to pick up the ball, set up the furniture and go around dribbling anything that popped in front of me.

That's how I spent my entire childhood at my grandparent's house, where I lived with my parents. We shared a small room – me, my sister and my parents. From the door, there was a mattress to the left, where we all four slept. In front of the mattress there was a trunk and a wardrobe. There was a small space between the mattress and the wardrobe, and it was in this narrow corridor that I used to play with the ball. And also on the mattress. That was my pitch. I used to love to kick the ball around and to then throw myself on the mattress as a goalie to make an outrageous save. Because it was such a narrow space, I could play as the goalie too.

My cousins also played. Well . . . I made them part of the game. Jennifer was one of the goal posts. Rafaela, my sister, was another post. Lorrayne and Rayssa were the opponents (actually, more like training dummies). They stood as obstacles, and sometimes even wore jerseys so I could pretend it was a real match. I would spend hours dribbling around them, learning to control the ball in that tight environment, always just me against them. Hours and hours and hours were spent like that. And in so doing, I became incredibly comfortable with the ball, I learned balance, and I learned how to negotiate my way through claustrophobic conditions. I felt complete with a ball at my feet; there is no other way to describe it.

I recently did a photo shoot for an ad campaign. When we finished, I asked for the ball we used, as I always do. I went to the elevators doing freestyle kick ups. Since there was nobody there, I continued for the whole trip down. At the lobby, a couple of kids asked for autographs. After a few pictures I continued to play with the ball all the way to my car. I tell you, I can't live without the ball. Ever since my grandparent's house. Ever since birth.

A few years later, when we had moved out and into the little house my father was able to build at Praia Grande, the 'pitch' was also very simple. One of the goals was on the back door. The other was in my room. I used to play my own games and competitions. I kicked the ball around, and did commentary of the games. I played, narrated and cheered. 'And then Neymar scored! Neymarzinho!' There were even fouls. When I dribbled and hit the sofa, I complained to the referee. Of course, it was all imaginary, but I played like it was for real. I miss that. It was the game at its purest.

I used to train by kicking a very small ball against the wall. When my right foot got tired, I switched to the left. Then, I started to use my right thigh. Then the left. And after that, I practised controlling the ball with my chest. Then my head. Not only to head goals, but also controlling the position of the ball. It wasn't easy. But it was all play. And, without even noticing, I was getting better.

I also developed my style a lot playing at the beach. When my father had the time, we used to kick the ball around there. He used to show me where and how to kick. He would touch my foot and say, 'This is where you hit the ball.' Then I had to repeat the lesson. I had to kick the ball with the part of the foot that he had pointed to.

But, of course, there was a day when I messed up. My father had built a really nice small pitch at home. He did it all by himself, even cultivating the beautiful green grass. One day, I invited my friends to spend the afternoon playing football with me. It had rained and the new grass hadn't fully rooted to the undersoil yet. And we completely ruined it. Once my friends went home I spent the rest of the evening imagining the row my father would give me as soon as he got home from work late that night and saw all that mud. I spent the following two weeks 'going to sleep early' so that I could avoid him. My father arrived home and found me 'sleeping' for days.

Besides ruining my father's pitch, I also liked to play manager. I would organise competitions, complete with groups, play-offs, semi-finals and finals. I spent so many hours playing and winning my imaginary games and competitions, dreaming of one day doing it for real.

I'll always remember my pitch at Praia Grande. Oh, how the neighbour's doors suffered! They were also some of our goals. And so were my mum's vases . . . Man, she used to really get angry with me for that. She would go nuts at home because I was always running around, kicking the ball everywhere and not always hitting the right spots. I guess I don't have to tell you what happened next.

As a mother who takes good care of everyone, she would ask me, 'Son, please don't do that.' But she never stopped me from playing. Quite the contrary: she encouraged me as much as my dad. Her father, my grandpa Arnaldo, also played football. I never met him, but I'm sure he was a fighter, just like my mum. She always did everything for us. Not only dealing with me at home, but also taking me to training and games when my dad couldn't, because he was working so hard in those days. I'm also very fortunate in that sense. My parents always did everything they could for me to be happy. Without my parents, this book wouldn't exist. This story would be just another boy's dream.

WORKING WITH HONOUR

THE LOVE THAT JUNINHO has for what he does is not just about the game: it's about the object. It's about the ball. You'd be amazed. He loves that instrument more than anything. That's why I always say he is first and foremost a ball player more than a footballer. And that's what it takes to become a world-class player. You must like the ball. You must love it, and show respect and admiration for it. You can only aspire to be a good professional if you know the fundamentals of your trade. More than that: if you love testing all the possibilities with the tools of your trade.

Typically, children are not in love with football. They are in love with the ball. They play in the living room, in the backyard, on the street, anywhere. It doesn't matter if it's a narrow space, if it may break something. The kid wants the ball, and wants to play with a toy that later can become something more serious, as happened with my son.

People who play football can tell a good player just by seeing his first touches on the ball. Mário Américo, a physio during the golden age of the Brazilian national team in the 1970s, used to say, 'You can tell an ace just by the way he walks.' I must say, I could tell Neymar Jr had it in him even before he learned to walk.

When he was three years old, I realised how far he might be able to go. It was supposed to be just father and son having some fun with a ball. But, for him, the ball was not just some toy. It was serious business. And he wasn't greedy: he always passed the ball back to me, and with great accuracy. Usually, kids just kick the ball and then play by themselves. Some even use their hands. But not Juninho. He played football. He wanted to communicate with me through the ball. He knew he needed someone to play with and exchange passes. He learned very easily, almost by instinct. Even in his first matches you could see he was different, not only because of his skills, but also for his vision of the game. When kids play, they usually all run together towards the ball and swarm around it, but Juninho would stay apart from that huddle, just waiting for the right opportunity.

Seeing his talent, I started to try more sophisticated passes with him. And the boy would react, control and pass the ball back in the right direction. I didn't even need to explain, he understood everything right away. He knew where to pass the ball and what to do with it.

Professionally, I played as a right winger. I was a good dribbler, but lacked the skills to score; I only scored a few goals in my career. My left foot was also weak. Like some in the game like to say, the left foot is only good for stepping on the bus, at best. However, Juninho wasn't like that. From the start, he could do everything and I could tell that he had great potential. He liked football so much that he started to collect balls. Eventually we had more than 50 at home, of all kinds: good and bad, old and new, flat and pumped up. His room was so full that you could barely walk inside. And he loved them all, especially the small ones that were more difficult to control.

I can't remember the first time I kicked a ball, and I know Juninho can't either. But when there's a single thing in life that we do, that we really want to and that we dream of, we can say we were born doing it. That's his relationship with football: it's a true love affair.

It's an affair I also used to have, but that was shaken by the car accident. It pretty much left me unable to walk for a whole year, shortening a career that would officially end in 1997, after I won the Mato Grosso state championship with Operário de Várzea Grande. In the final game, we beat União de Rondonópolis, 2-1. It was 3 August 1997. There was big party, and I retired soon after.

In early 1998, less than six months after my last game, I applied for a job at CET (the Traffic Engineering Company) in Santos. Since I had always liked cars and worked a lot at my father's garage, I thought CET would be good place to begin my life away from the sport.

I was accepted and got the job – but not to work with cars, as I wanted. It was a job as a construction worker. CET was changing all the bus stops in Santos, and I was just another worker building the new shelters on the streets. I fixed pavements, dug holes for the posts, and things like that.

It was not the kind of work I wanted, but it was what I could do. After four months of hard work, I moved to a better job within the company. CET used to outsource their vehicle maintenance, and since I was good with mechanics, I covered for a friend of mine, Juvenal, when he went on holiday. I did well while he was away and soon started to take care of all the motorbikes from the Military Police and CET. I eventually became maintenance chief and only left that job in 2009, when I dropped everything to manage my son's career. And, God willing, he will have a better end to his career than I did – after all, I went from state champion to construction worker in the blink of an eye.

They were both dignified and honourable jobs, but totally different to each other. I was the family's breadwinner, and I earned minimum wage. So, I also started to sell Panasonic water purifiers to make ends meet. I had to improvise. Imagine what it's like for me to see my son in adverts nowadays for the same company. Who would have thought something like that would happen?

I worked very hard for my family. I never had it easy financially as an athlete, but I was able to contribute to my son's dream. When I started at CET I also did various odd jobs on the side to earn extra income. I used an old Volkswagen Type 2 to make transportations here and there. When we hit a bend in the road, people in the back had to hold the door so it wouldn't fly open. Doing that, I met two fellows who owned amateur sports clubs in Praia Grande. One of them, Toninho, worked as a customs broker and had a football pitch in Jardim Real. The other was a contractor called Jura, who owned a club at Melvi.

I had a plot of 12 by 30 metres in Praia Grande. It was all I had left from my career as a professional athlete, and my dream was to build a little house for my wife and kids on it. I didn't have any money to buy construction materials so this dream felt a long way off.

But I have been blessed in this life with some wonderful friends. Toninho got me all the materials I needed. And Jura hired some builders to erect the house – all in exchange for playing for their amateur teams. On Saturdays I played for one team, and on Sundays I played for the other. Those two men helped me a lot. And they still do. Thanks to them I was able to build the house of my dreams.

I have been through many difficult times. There was an occasion when we had no money to pay the electricity bill and we were cut off. The funny thing is that Juninho and Rafaela were amused by the situation. Unlike the adults, they couldn't wait for night-time, when we lit all the candles. They loved it. I couldn't complain. After all, what we had in that house with no electricity was priceless: true love. That's how you really build a home, a life. With love. With tenderness. With partnership. With patience. Even without money, our family was united and happy.

After I quit football, I still received invitations to play professionally, but the contracts were based on me staying injury-free and it was too much of a gamble. I would have been one bad tackle away from instantly losing my job and plunging my family into poverty. It wasn't a risk I could take. As much as I wished that I could still play professional football, there was no way back. Saying no to those offers was incredibly painful, but the reality was that for the sake of financial security and the wellbeing of my family, I had to do it. I had to let go of my dreams and keep it real. But doing so was more painful than any injury I'd ever suffered on the pitch.

There were times when I went home from CET crying my eyes out. Not because of my job, but for the football I couldn't play professionally anymore. It was a pain similar to when you lose a competition, or an important game, but it was even worse, since I was no longer on the pitch. I had to fight somewhere else, in some other way, for me and for my family. As a man who hates to lose, not being able to compete at all is worse still.

The game of life can be cruel, but you shouldn't ever give up. Never stop dreaming. I've never stopped. To this day I keep dreaming, and I allow my children to do the same.

THE ETERNAL SANTOS FC

I CAN REMEMBER SEEING my father playing in amateur competitions when I was six years old. One thing that stuck out was how desperately he desperately wanted to win, how relentlessly competitive he was. I learned a lot watching him and I soon came to understand that to get results, you need to train and play with total commitment at all times.

Even though I was just a kid, I soon learned not to dribble aimlessly, to be aware of the responsibility of being in possession of the ball and to always respect your opponent. My father is always telling me, 'Keep moving, son. Never stop, move to both sides and let the opponent get tired. Don't stay in your comfort zone, don't make the opposition's life easier.' He showed me how some highly skilled players can lose themselves in pointless dribbles or waste time showing off their skills with little benefit for their team. They carry the ball to the sidelines, they do kick-ups in the middle of the field, but they never score. How many times has this excessive behaviour ended up hurting the team's performance? Not to mention complaints from teammates, criticism from the coach and anger from the fans. My father and I used to spend hours analysing this kind of thing.

To win, you need to do your best. While it is important to feel the same joy as you would in an amateur, friendly match, at the same time you need to be aware of everything that constitutes being a professional footballer. Most clubs are well-established institutions with proud histories that you are now representing, and there are fans, sponsors and commercial partners that believe in and support your work.

I was fortunate enough to have all of that from the day I joined Santos FC. The great Zito, from the legendary team of the 50s and 60s, was the one who brought me to the club. After playing for Gremetal and Tumiaru in São Vicente, Mr Zito saw me playing futsal and did all he could to take me from Portuguesa Santista to Santos FC. I'm forever grateful for his trust in me and for all his efforts.

I played futsal from the age of seven until I was 12, and started to play association football after that.

Even though I was skinny and quite small, I always played in the age groups above my own. It was a great way to gain experience. At the age of seven, I played with ten-year-old kids. At the age of nine, I played with teenagers, and so on. But the the downside was encountering the grown men playing in lower age groups, the kind of ridiculous scenario that can sometimes happen in football. They used to tackle me very hard, trying to intimidate me. We used to jokingly say that some under-15 players had their own sons watching the match. It was hard to believe they were only 15 years old. However, there was always some teammate or coach to help me. Our coach, Mr Lima, a great player from Pelé's team, would often speak with my father and me about that. I remember one day he came up to me after a match to see if I was okay, saying I had been beaten up by 'a 32-year-old playing for the under-15 squad.' It was funny, but I did suffer a lot with the physicality of those games.

At that time, Santos didn't have an under-13 squad so, at a suggestion from Mr Zito, they created an under-13 team so that I and other kids could begin to play for the club. That was great in every aspect and as a result I started to receive a real salary and could bring a little money back home.

In the beginning, when I was seven years old, I was given a basket of household items in exchange for playing. When the schools were able to invest, they started to offer scholarships. And the best thing was that everything was doubled, since my father was a great negotiator and was able to get everything for me and my sister. He was even able to negotiate a petrol allowance for my coach, Betinho. Since my father and mother had to work, Betinho used to drive me to Santos FC. Actually, not just me, but also other children who lived nearby. After a day of study and training he used to say to us, 'Now, you boys rest, okay?' Yeah, right . . . We would wait until he was gone and then go out to play in the street, at home, wherever we could. We just loved the game so much.

The investment from the Santos FC President, Marcelo Teixeira, in the Meninos da Vila training centre was critical for my future at Santos, and for the discovery of other talents. There's nothing better than working somewhere that you love, that feels like home. I felt very comfortable at Santos, having joined when I was 11. I was one of the boys. My only concern there was to play football, the club took care of everything else and did everything they could to ensure that I was happy. In that crazy routine of training, studying, travelling, and playing, I needed someone at home to give me support. My father, even though he was with me as often as he could be, still worked for CET. So, thanks to the financial help from Santos, my mother was able to stay at home to take care of me.

One of the best things in football is to experience a sense of belonging, a feeling of 'all for one and one for all' among the players and the fans, and across an entire organisation. That is something I have been lucky enough to experience with Santos, the Seleção, and now Barcelona.

My father says I am a fan as much as I am a player, and I do feel this way even when I'm on the pitch, which is great. I want to give myself to the teams I love, as if I were a fan watching from the stands. And the best thing is, both with Santos and Barcelona, their philosophy has always been to support their own prodigies, those players who grew up inside the clubs, as best they can. This creates a great sense of affinity with the club, which helps to build a passion for success both on and off the field.

When you play for a team you love, you don't simply want to win matches. You want to please your own people, your fans, your club. And so everything you do is driven by a great emotion. We want to win games and win over the crowd. We want to make our fans proud. Great squads formed within a club are not just winning teams: they are teams everyone likes to see. It's like homemade food: it always has more flavour, more love.

This is a winning recipe. It happened to me with Santos. And I can see the same passion and ambition at Barcelona.

REAL MADRID

ONEY DOESN'T FORGIVE FOOLISHNESS. You have to save. That's why I take care of my son's earnings with great caution. I have to give him freedom so he can shine. Neymar Jr needs to play football. I take care of the bureaucracy so that he can concentrate on doing that to the best of his abilities. He's not worried about how much he's making, but I am. And I work so he can thrive as successfully off the pitch as he does on it.

It is not greed, it is responsibility. I want the best for my son, for his family, for our family. That's why I work so hard for him, in the same way he works hard for us. Shortly after he became a professional for Santos FC, in 2009, he started to become inundated with offers, so I realised that I had to start exerting a more controlling influence over proceedings so that he could be guided in the best way possible. When the big money began to roll in I knew we had to be cautious. The world of sport and entertainment is full of stories of young men and women living to wild excess and blowing every penny that they have earned with nothing to show for it afterwards and often with their reputations in tatters. To play football, you need to be grounded and keep your head clear. You can't be blinded by the money you make when you're so young; you need to be cautious every step of the way. At the age of 11, Neymar Jr signed a contract with Santos. We valued that a lot: it was an acknowledgment of the regard that Santos had for my son. And money isn't more important than that. In 2006, he could've become a Real Madrid player. But he didn't want it. We didn't want it.

Wagner Ribeiro, our agent, brought us the proposal. Wagner, who was first introduced to us by Betinho, is a successful and well-respected agent who was impressed by Juninho's talent very early in his career. When my son was 12 years old, we signed with Uruguayan agent Juan Figer, who was also famous in footballing circles. He and Marcel Figer, his son, started to take care of Neymar Jr and then handed over responsibility for his career to Wagner, who was the Figers' business partner at their agency. We closed the deal with Santos, and started to earn a little money every month.

It wasn't much. But with my salary from CET and the financial help Santos offered so Juninho would stay, we had a lift in our quality of life and my wife was able to quit her job.

Things were starting to look up, until Wagner Ribeiro had a disagreement with Santos because of the long negotiation between Robinho, another of his clients, and Real Madrid. People even started to say that Juninho would have to leave Santos if Wagner was still our agent. That was hard. Neymar Jr was giving his best in training and in matches and some people wanted to take him out of the club just because Wagner was working with me. It was completely absurd.

I didn't think it was fair, because Wagner was helping us a lot. I learned a great deal from him, and I often visited him at his office. He had taken a bet on my son very early in the process, and he was looking out for us. It was not right to stop working with him because of pressure from the club. We couldn't just ditch him so we could be better off. We had nothing to do with his problems with Santos, and vice versa. And, above all, we had a deal with our agent, and we wanted to stand by our word. That is more valuable than anything. It is with loyalty that you win at anything in life.

When Juninho was 13 years old, Wagner pitched his CV to Real Madrid. We travelled by plane for the first time and spent 19 days in Spain. Real Madrid made a proposal similar to that which Barcelona had made to Lionel Messi when he was a kid. It was a bet for the future. They would take Neymar Jr to Madrid and he would grow up in Spain, as a man and an athlete. The financial offer was quite extraordinary considering that he was just a young teenager.

But just six days into our trip to Europe, my son and I couldn't take anymore. Everything just felt too different for us. On these occasions, you have to trust your paternal instinct. I've had many struggles in my life. I'm an adult, a grown man, but my son was still just a kid and I could sense that he felt overwhelmed by it all. He had grown up in a small house where four of us had shared a bedroom for much of his childhood. Even though I was in Spain with him, I could tell that he felt completely out of his comfort zone. Sometimes being pushed like that can be hugely beneficial, but sometimes it can be equally detrimental.

To send him to Europe, even with the huge earnings on offer and the potential for bigger and better things in time, would have been too traumatic for him. As father and agent to my son, I had to think long-term and of all the consequences, and not simply be wooed by the riches that were being laid before us. I had to measure everything. Every decision that you make will have good and bad sides. Nothing is 100% or 0%. You have to balance things. You have to know that, sometimes, turning something down does not necessarily mean that you are losing things. You're just choosing not to get them at that particular moment. I felt that that was an important attitude to take at that juncture of Juninho's career.

That's what happened when we went to Madrid. We could have been living in Europe since 2006, but it is gratifying to look at all that Neymar Jr has achieved with both Santos and Brazil since turning down Real's offer. It was a risk, of course, but when I look back now I am satisfied that we made the right choices at the right time for his career. But it wasn't easy to say no. On his first day in Madrid, he went straight to training. And how well he played! After 19 days, he had scored 27 goals in various training sessions. Within the first three days, we had agreed on everything with the club. The contract was written, all seemed well. Juninho and Rafaela were to receive scholarships. The only thing missing was the signature from his mother. Nadine had a plane ticket to come to Europe with me and Juninho, but she had chosen to stay at home with our Rafaela.

But a few days later, less than a week after our arrival, Juninho didn't seem well. He was homesick. He missed our family, his friends, his school, his city, and Santos FC. He missed everything. I saw Neymar Jr become sadder with each day that passed. The air was getting heavier. Even with everything being done to make us feel comfortable and welcome, I just felt that the moment wasn't right. And Juninho agreed. So we decided to fly back to Santos. We were happy to return home. Our hearts decided it and I didn't even care how much money we were turning down. All I wanted was for him to continue to play with joy. And there was no joy for him in Madrid in those days, and no money could ever change that.

Our decision was based on how Juninho felt. As a father, I realised his situation and told Wagner Ribeiro and Mr Zito, at Santos, that we wanted to come back. Santos' coach at the time, Vanderlei Luxemburgo, who had worked with Real Madrid in 2005, also wanted him to stay. He called Wagner and they convinced President Marcelo Teixeira to invest in Juninho. We were sure that we would have other offers during his career. It was neither the time nor the place. I felt that Neymar Jr needed to mature at Santos, playing competitions in Brazil first. One day he would go to Europe to learn even more. But first he needed to grow up in our home, in our country.

Many people called and came to talk with us. They thought I was crazy for rejecting a proposal from Europe and a club like Real Madrid. Many people thought we had missed the opportunity of a lifetime.

But, of course, to stay in Santos we needed to negotiate a better deal for ourselves; so we called Marcelo Teixeira. He invited us to a meeting at Universidade Santa Cecília. We talked, and fortunately everything went well.

At 13 years old, Neymar Jr was already a successful youth player and the club believed in his future. With the new deal in place we were able to leave our house in Praia Grande and buy a better apartment. Santos FC was really our home and the first apartment we bought was in front of the club.

It turned out to be the right choice for us. We are grateful to all those who interceded and helped us, especially Mr Zito. Now, just between us, when Juninho signed that contract in our old house at Praia Grande, I was hoping Mr Zito would buy us a big lunch at some fancy restaurant, as a courtesy from the club. Fat chance. He only ate the *empadas* [a kind of pasty] leftover from Juninho's birthday!

Mr Zito, what a great man. A dear friend to our family. Even when he says that if he could play against Neymar he would . . . Well, I better not say how I think that would have ended had it ever happened!

I AM NEYMAR JR

WHEN I'M WITH MY friends, I realise I still have the soul of a child. Of course, I also know that I have responsibilities. I am a professional footballer and I became a father when I was 19 years old. But I often feel like a grown child, always wanting to play with a ball in the street, laugh with friends, and play video games. I was born a simple man, and I will die the same way. As for food, I like the basics: a very simple Brazilian meal with rice, beans, fries and *farofa* [a toasted manioc flour mixture, similar in appearance to couscous]. What else do you need? Oh, right – biscuits. I love biscuits. And ice cream . . . I had an industrial refrigerator installed in my office just to keep a stash of ice cream handy.

As for my wardrobe, I like to change things up every now and then. And I make no exceptions when I do: I change everything, from my hair to my shoes to my accessories. But there's one thing I don't take much care of: my playing jerseys. I don't keep many jerseys because I'm always promising them to my friends. Sometimes I just plain forget about them. If it weren't for the kit staff at Barcelona, I would have forgotten the jersey I wore when I was first introduced to the fans at Camp Nou. I just left everything in the changing room afterwards. Actually, it's not just jerseys. I'm also very forgetful of my trophies. I left the one I received at the 2012 London Olympics in my hotel room. And I left another trophy at a hotel in Argentina – this time after we won the Copa América [the competition contested every four years to decide the continental champion of South America; it is the oldest international continental football competition in the world]. It may sound careless, but in many ways it is because these items are trappings of my job, not my main focus.

The only thing I never turn off is my passion. I live and breathe football 24-7, either playing or watching. I like to review plays from other players so I can absorb them. I really like to watch freestyle exhibitions so I can update my own tricks. Freestyle football is a sport where the players performs various tricks, including balancing the ball on various parts of the body. I like to learn from these guys and adapt their moves or use them as inspiration to create my own. It's funny, I can recall just about every special move I've ever played in a match. I think it's very important to remember moves, goals, matches, so you can always get better and better. They are reference points from which you can learn, adapt and seek to improve.

My passions have remained the same since I was a child and that's perhaps why I often still feel so like a young boy. When it's time to relax, my joy depends on football. If my team loses or if I didn't play well, then I just stay quiet at home. I play snooker, video games, or cards, alone at home. If my friends aren't with me, then we all meet online. In these moments, it's better to just stay at home, relax and refocus on the next challenge and how to bounce back from the disappointment of the loss.

However, if my team wins . . . Well, then it's time to celebrate. I like to go out to dance with my friends and just have a good time. I love music and I listen to everything: funk, samba, *pagode*, black music, gospel music, whatever is on the menu. I just can't live without music. I have an aunt who is a singer, and an uncle who is a music producer. My grandpa, my grandma, everyone at home breathes music. They all like samba and *pagode*. And I just love it all.

Then there's me and the guys from *tóis*. Many people ask me what this '*tóis*' thing is that we're always talking about. Well, it all began with a friend of ours, the brother-in-law of Gabriel, a winger from SC Internacional. He started jokingly saying *tóis* instead of *nóis*, which in Portuguese means something like 'we all' or 'our gang'. It was all a joke, but it somehow became our motto. Everything is *tóis* now. It's just a joke, but it caught on.

But there's one place where my talents aren't welcome, and that is the karaoke stage. I'm a loud and lousy singer. But, honestly, I couldn't care less. I like to sing! If people don't like it, they can leave. Except that, well, some people actually do leave!

I also love to travel and get to know other countries and cultures. But, having said that, I don't particularly like the travelling part of it. I have very little patience for the number of hours we spend inside airplanes. Time passes and it feels like you're not moving at all. So I try to sleep – and I'm very good at it, too. There was one time when we hit very strong turbulence and people started to pray and cry. But I slept like a log. Then, when they woke me, I saw all those scared faces and asked what happened. They couldn't believe that I had managed to sleep through it all.

I'm a relaxed guy. Mostly because I have wonderful friends to share everything with. Many of my current friends I met only four, five years ago, but there is a small group from my early childhood and from school who I still see. I had many more when I was younger, but we naturally lost contact, I guess. And since my life is so crazy right now, it's hard to find the time to see everyone. But the friends I have today are the most important to me and I always try to be with them, in both good and in bad times.

I love telling jokes, and I know a lot of good ones. But my friends don't agree that much. They say they're repetitive and dull. But that's because they're always with me, so they listen to the same old stories again and again!

One of my great pleasures is to ride my bike along Santos' shore. I used to cycle to training at Santos FC on my bike, and when I am back there, I put on a cap and just go out cycling.

I also like tattoos – so much so that I'm beginning to lose track of all the ones I have. One day I went to the mall in Santos, and visited one of those studios with a big glass window. In no time, there was a small crowd watching as the tattoo artist drew on my skin. I like that kind of attention. Although, the process of *getting* the tattoo isn't that nice. But I guess it's worth the message. I have the name of my son, Davi Lucca, and his birthday tattooed on my arm. I also have the word 'blessed' (in English) near the back of my neck. I have the names of my mother and sister on each of my arms. '*Deus é fiel*' (God is faithful) appears on my left wrist, '*ousadia*' (boldness) on my left ankle, and '*alegria*' (joy) on my right ankle. I also have a crown, a heart, the infinity symbol, and the passage Corinthians 9:24:27 in Portuguese. And, of course, one of my tattoos, on my chest, had to be a tribute to my greatest idol: my father.

BOYISH BEHAVIOUR?

I STRONGLY FEEL THAT modesty is essential for a happy life. That's why I have always tried to guide Neymar Jr in things outside the sport. Yes, he likes to have an edgy look, but I have always tried to keep him grounded. When he was younger, I was very strict with him. Now that he is an adult, a father and a homeowner, he knows the choices that he makes are his own and he must be happy to live by them. Ever since he was a child, and with all the attention he received from everyone at Santos and from other clubs, I always tried to make sure he didn't live too extravagantly.

I've always been strict because I felt that that is a father's role. In many situations, saying no is actually an act of love. There's no greater love than that which a parent has for their child. We love our children even before they are born. We may cease to be a lot of thing in life, but we never cease to be parents.

Nobody wants to forbid anything just for the sake of it. We

do it because we feel we are doing it for the best interests of our children. Juninho sees no problem in wearing earrings and 'working on his looks'. But I believe that this kind of audacious apparel may get more attention than his talent as a footballer, and that shouldn't happen. The quality of a professional is measured by his performance on the pitch, and also by the professional image that he projects.

Having a strong personality is a good thing. However, you shouldn't be individualistic. Neymar Jr learned this very early in life. That's also why he's good with team sports. He never wanted to be more than anyone else. He never thought of himself as better than his teammates or opponents. That's an essential attitude to have in your profession and in life.

A little criticism here and there can turn around any bad behaviour or curtail bad habits. Since he started playing futsal and football, I have always talked with him a lot – during the bus journeys, or sometimes on my motorcycle. I used to talk about his behaviour, what he should do with the ball and what he shouldn't do. I always reviewed the before and the after in each of his matches. And I was never too soft. I never focused only on the good parts. It's easy to sugar-coat everything, but what lessons can you learn if you take that approach? The truth is that you also need to show the ugly side of life.

Nobody should take to the pitch thinking they can't lose. Being arrogant is the worst way to lose a match. And that applies to every aspect of life.

I'll never forget the time I was working at CET and one day I was called to clean the women's bathroom. That was not part of the deal when I was hired. I wanted to work with cars, not clean anyone's bathroom. But I was determined to do the best cleaning I could, so I gave my best and left the place spotless, so much so that some supervisors didn't want me to leave the job. I almost became chief of bathroom cleaning.

Of course, I didn't want that. Not that there's anything wrong with that – quite the contrary, I have respect for all professions. But I wanted other things. To achieve my goal, I needed to do my best at that job and show my value to my employers. I always want to give my best, and I have taught my children the same lessons.

One time, at a training session at Gremetal, Neymar Jr ended a play by kicking the ball with his left foot, his weak foot. The result was horrible. His coach, Betinho, took him aside and told him that in situations like that he should always kick with his right foot.

With all due respect to Betinho, I thought the exact opposite. I said to Juninho, 'Son, you should kick with the foot next to the ball, whichever it is. Don't be afraid to use your weak foot. Use it once, twice, three times, until the weak foot is not weak anymore. Until you feel it's strong. The weak leg also helps the strong leg.'

After that I talked with Betinho and asked him to insist that Neymar Jr also kicked with the weak leg, even if the kick was not too good at first. This was his time to learn, when he was seven, eight years old. The real mistake would be to stop improving. He shouldn't be afraid of trying and taking risks.

Betinho was always a great coach and a humble person. Not only did he accept what I thought was best for my son, but he also started to apply the same strategy with his other students. And to this day I think the same way. With the right degree of intervention, you can change an entire trajectory, an entire attitude, an entire way of thought.

Juninho then started to work hard on developing his left foot. And he got it wrong many, many times – until he started to get it more right than wrong, like in the final match of the 2013 Confederations Cup at the Maracaná in Rio. [The Confederations Cup is held every four years and is contested by the holders of each of the six FIFA confederation championships – UEFA, CONMEBOL, CONCACAF, CAF, AFC, OFC – along with the FIFA World Cup holder and the host nation. It is held in the nation that will host the FIFA World Cup in the following year; Brazil were the 2013 hosts in advance of hosting the World Cup in 2014.] That goal against Spain, finished by a superb left-footed strike against Iker Casillas, was started in those training sessions with Betinho at Gremetal.

One thing is crucial in the life of a young man: the mentor, the instructor, the guy who teaches you. To be able to contribute as much as I could to Juninho's career, I went to college to study Physical Education. I wanted to learn everything I could so that I could try to teach even more about football, and sports in general, to Juninho. So I could keep up with him. As we say in Brazil, being a father is not enough, you have to participate.

Oh, and of course, you have to be patient with those who expect too much of your son or, in some cases, know too little about football. Many times I have had to silently count in my head to keep calm while listening to people criticise our team and our players in TV and radio broadcasts, or while reading similar reports in the press. I know criticism is part of the game, but sometimes it is hard to listen to some stuff, like people saying that my son is a choker. I have to tolerate it, but it's not easy. I always asked Juninho to never run away from the responsibility of carrying the team, and to always move infield looking for work. And he has always done that. Even when he doesn't play so well, he never shies away from doing his duty of fighting for the ball and giving options to his teammates.

I always stand by the ones I love, not just my son. I stand by those who play football. I remember one of the last games that the great Giovanni played for Santos, a fan shouted that he was too slow. I couldn't contain myself and I argued with the guy. Politely, of course, but I couldn't hold back anymore. How could he say that a top player like him was too slow? He had been one of the best I'd ever seen playing for Santos. And it was an incredible moment when Juninho played against him. At the end of the game, the two of them shared a hug. It was wonderful to see the encounter between those two generations.

For me, that moment was even more significant. I could see my son's burgeoning talents emerging while Giovanni was still shining with Santos FC and the Seleção, and then with Barcelona (a curious parallel, isn't it?). At times like that, I would remember the matches that Juninho had played with the Santos youth team, and how far he had come. Some days, there would be around ten opposing fans watching, and only me and a friend of mine, Zeferino, rooting for Santos. Zeferino had a bar in front of CET, where I worked, and he had also been a footballer when he was younger. We became close friends because of football.

I never missed one of the youth team games, and Zeferino was always with me. He used to drive me to all the stadiums in São Paulo. And we had to get up really early, because some games would start at nine o'clock. But we were always there, beside Juninho, right in the first row. We were never late to a game, and sometimes even got there before the arrival of the team bus. I used to call Zeferino very early in the morning, because it wasn't always easy to find the stadiums. We visited São Caetano, Mauá, Barueri. Sometimes we got lost and not even the locals knew where the stadium was. But we never missed a game, and that's because we knew: Juninho was going to make it. Big time.

THE DEBUT

UNTIL MY DEBUT FOR Santos on 7 March 2009, my father used to say that Juninho was his son. After the match against Oeste de Itápolis, at the Pacaembu Stadium, he said he had just become the father of Neymar Jr. He was incredibly proud. He had managed to guide me into Santos' first team. Now, it was up to me to realise the dreams that he hadn't.

My first-team debut lifted a huge weight from his shoulders, and, of course, from mine, too. The decision to stay at Santos three years earlier had made me so happy at the time, but it had been a big decision for the family, financially as much as anything else. We secured a great deal from the club when I returned from Spain, for which we will always be grateful, but there was a lot of talk about a deal like that being made with such a young player and the expectations of me were enormous. The media circus was already in full swing, ready to see if I would live up to my billing or not. The fans also shared in this sense of anticipation and were hopeful that with the new generation, which included Robinho and Diego, the club would enjoy another golden chapter in its history. As much as I had prepared myself since I was 11 for this day (and dreamed about it when I was even younger), it's something entirely different when you're standing in the tunnel before the match, waiting to be called on to the field.

When I started paying football it was all about fun and games and just the sheer joy of playing with the ball at my feet; from the moment I joined the professional team the responsibility settled in. I had to prove myself not just to myself and to my family, but to my teammates, the coaches and the management. And the press. And the fans. And the opponents. And everyone else. 'Let's see if this Neymar guy is as good as everyone is saying.'

It's not easy. And it hasn't become any easier as the years go by, particularly for my father. There are matches where he struggles to contain himself when he hears someone over-criticise me, especially when they target my personal life rather than the technical aspects of my play. But I guess all fathers are like that.

While not being conceited enough to want to draw any direct comparisons, my father has reminded me that not even Pelé had as much attention when he made his debut. I think few people ever had. After I turned down the offer from Real Madrid in 2006, everyone knew who I was. And after that, even when playing for the youth team, I had at least one request per game for photographs from the fans. That was not normal for someone my age. But I had to get used to it.

There is no doubt that this rise in my profile opened a lot of doors for me. However, football always has its hard moments –

just like life. Santos was going through a transitional phase in 2009 with a new manager, Vágner Mancini, and so it took a while for me to actually make my debut. Mancini made a good start to his reign, beating São Paulo 1-0. We hadn't beaten a major team for nine months, and we hadn't beaten São Paulo in the Campeonato Paulista since the year 2000. Things were starting to look up and it was a wonderful moment when, during this match, the fans started to shout my name while I was on the bench, imploring Mancini to put me on. It was an unforgettable feeling.

But despite the pressure, and everything that my family and I had gone through, my debut felt more like a victory than a burden. It was Saturday night. The match began at 7.10 p.m. Fifteen minutes into the second half, I finally came off the bench to replace the Colombian midfielder Molina. There were almost 24,000 fans packed into the stadium, a great crowd, as there usually is when Santos play in the capital. The fans were so supportive when I stepped onto the field, it was great. It could've been even better, because with my first touch of the ball I hit the post; it was disappointing to miss, of course, but our victory was more important than me scoring. We won 2-1 and I had great fun in my debut, and that was very important to me. I felt relaxed, and like I belonged out there.

After that first match, it was time for my debut at our home stadium. We played Paulista the following week and again I came off the bench in the second half, this time replacing the defender Domingos. I played well, but by the end of the game I was still to score and to be in the starting team.

After the thrill of the debut and also the first match at home, I had a clear objective: to score for the first time, and for that goal to be the first of many I would score for Santos.

And it happened on 15 March 2009, on a Sunday night at the Pacaembu Stadium. I was 17 years old. My teammate Ganso (the press still called him Paulo Henrique at the time) scored the first goal of the night against Mogi Mirim, 12 minutes into the second half. Roni, a wild guy, scored with a header ten minutes later. Then, in the 27th minute of the second half, there was a passage of great play down the left side of the field, Roni escaped into space and then crossed the ball infield towards the goal. I was free and jumped to meet the ball with a diving header and fired it past the Mogri Mirim keeper. 3-0! There I was, skinny as it gets, wearing the beautiful number seven jersey.

Just before I made my first-team debut for Santos, my grandpa had passed away. Seu Ilzemar had been a huge fan of Pelé's. When I was a kid I used to sit with my grandpa and watch videos of the King; we would study his plays and rejoice in his goals and the way he celebrated. My father was much the same, he always talked about how much he loved Pelé's famous fist pump in the air after he scored. So when I scored I didn't think twice; I wheeled away and punched the air in the same style. Nobody will ever be at Pelé's level, but it was a tribute and in so doing I felt that I was able to pay homage to my grandpa and to my father. That goal and the celebration were for the two of them.

Thanks to God, my grandpa and my father, that goal was the first of many. Scoring gives you an indescribable feeling. It may be a goal that decides a match, a goal against a rival team, a sole goal in a defeat, a beautiful goal, a clumsy goal, a lucky goal, with the foot, with the head, with anything. There is no such thing as an ugly goal. Dario Maravilha, one of the greatest Brazilian strikers, used to have a phrase that my father loved: 'There is no ugly goal. Ugly is no goals at all.'

That's it. There's no better feeling for the fans, either – and every player was once a fan. Or still is, like me. I'm still the same guy who once watched the matches from the stands or on TV. Except that now I'm on the pitch and I can score for the team. When I do, I'm so happy that I can't help but celebrate like crazy.

I don't even want to imagine what my last goal will be like. Against which team, what year, what competition. Probably I won't even know it is the last one. However, with the first, I knew exactly what was happening. To this day I can't find the words to properly describe that moment or how to truly thank all those who helped me get to that point in my life and who were with me that day at the stadium. It is a moment that will live with me for the rest of my life.

EAGER TO WIN

ONE OF THE PSYCHOLOGISTS who worked with Neymar Jr said that, besides his talent, he has something that all great athletes have: an enormous, self-driven motivation. He derives such joy from playing football and making a living doing what he loves that he has never taken for granted how privileged he is. He has always been focused on improving himself and knows that the only way to do that is to work extremely hard. He knew that a dedication to self-improvement was the only way to push himself into the ranks of the elite, and is what he must to continue to do if he wants to make it to the very top of the game. With the talent God gave him, plus his ferocious work ethic, he's got everything required to be successful.

Juninho looks up to many great masters that inspire him: Messi, Cristiano Ronaldo, Robinho, Ronaldo, Xavi, Iniesta, Rivaldo, Romário, Zidane, and so many others. I know many kids now have him as their hero. That's one of the reasons he needs to be well prepared for everything. And in his case, that's not that hard, because he loves what he does so much.

You don't get tired when you do what you love. And Neymar Jr never gets tired of training and playing. Even with the seemingly thousand daily activities that are required of a professional athlete, Juninho is always the first to show up to training. He's always able and willing to learn, but he's not there just to perfect new skills and plays. He spends as much time on the pitch as he can because that's where he likes to be, where he feels most comfortable. It's in football that he feels most at home.

He never bought into the idea that 'training is not the same thing as a match'. To Juninho, a training session is of equal importance and status as a match. And a match is everything to a professional footballer. You have to work your hardest, but never disrespect others or go overboard with your competitive attitude. It's not a war. I always asked him to be the last to leave training, to give all he could in every way. If the match becomes stagnant, if he is too still, I will tell him that he has to inject energy into the play, he has to start to run everywhere and be the catalyst, to create momentum for his team. It is hard work, but he has to do it for his teammates.

A lot of people have criticised him over the years for falling too much, saying that he throws himself to the ground. But I watch these moments closely and often he is forced into jumping or else he risks the opponent breaking him. A stick in the air doesn't break. But that's the price of being a striker: the tackles are always hard. But we should mention that this only happens after the game starts, because in the moments before kick-off, all the opponents and the referees are friendly towards Neymar Jr.

They all respect not only his talent and professionalism, but also his humble spirit.

Success has not gone to his head. He might sport all kinds of crazy hairdos but inside he carries a great sense of responsibility. And that's how you win a lot more than just competitions and awards. The affection and respect from fans and colleagues is far more important to him. Before being a world class player, you need to be a good person. And Juninho has understood that ever since he was a little boy.

THE FANS

I'VE ALWAYS BEEN AN easy-going and relaxed guy, but I'm a little shy and I like to spend time on my own when I can. So it took a while for me learn how to deal with everything that comes with being a famous footballer. I have achieved some incredible things and, although it doesn't always sit comfortably, to be considered an idol by thousands, maybe even millions, of fans, is very special. It is a wonderful feeling to be popular and well known, but all my achievements, professionally and in my personal life, have been realised thanks to humility and dedication, and that is a lesson I shall never forget.

I confess that it took me a while to understand this crazy thing that is fame. To be honest, I'm still not sure that I really understand it. Sometimes I catch myself thinking that I must really be doing something special as an athlete to merit so much attention. Most of the time I don't really think about it because I'm so focused on just training and playing. Sometimes it's bewildering, but also very rewarding. With that, my responsibility grows even greater. I feel that I constantly need to surpass my previous accomplishments in order to deserve all that affection. Some people might think of me as a superstar, just because I'm famous. But I'm no better than anyone else.

I remember realising that things had changed one night in 2010. It was a Tuesday afternoon after a training session, and I decided to go to the mall to buy a music player. I was parking my car and I noticed that somebody recognised me. When I stepped out, there was suddenly a group of around ten people that just appeared around me, asking for autographs and pictures. I started to give the autographs and a big line formed right there in the car park. I thanked everyone, put my cap on, and walked quickly into the mall. But people followed me.

When I reached the store, a great crowd formed outside. The mall security and the manager had to come up with an evasive security operation on the fly. Doors were closed and I was able to buy what I wanted before they escorted me out through the back of the shop. I don't even know how I got out of there.

After all the commotion, one of the security guards advised me to come back on a less crowded day. I hadn't realised that it was a holiday and the mall was packed. That was the last time I went shopping by myself. That's one of the prices you pay in this career. At first, I didn't understand it all. It was different, and a bit scary. Some girls would cry so much when they saw me. And suddenly there were lots of kids sporting the same hairstyle I had. All this affection is rewarding, but it did scare me a little at the time. I never really imagined it could happen to me. It is one part of being a professional footballer that I had never aspired to experience; it has always been the game that has captured my dreams and imagination. But as time goes on, you get used to the attention and just have to accept that it comes with the job.

There was one occasion in January 2012 when I was playing footvolley with some friends at the beach. The boundary lines ended up being formed by the crowd around us. There were so many people! It was not easy to get out of there, I'll tell you.

There was also the time when I went to a drive-through. I rolled down the window and the woman at the till recognised me. In a matter of seconds, my car was surrounded by people, the majority of them kids. I signed a lot of autographs and posed for a heap of photos. It was fun, at least for me, but I guess the huge line of cars waiting behind me didn't like it so much, so I had to politely put an end to that impromptu signing session and move away to grab my meal.

But I understand the other side. I'll never forget the day I met the King, Pelé. I was sleeping in the club dorm, in 2009. I woke up to hear Tigrinho, our left winger, shouting, 'Pelé is here!' I got up really fast and started to run with my friend André. All we wanted to do was to get close to him. I almost lost my voice. It was such a thrill! He is a King in everything. He's very polite to everyone, and he talks to you as if he knows you, always with a friendly word. It's almost like he's not from this world. But then, after all, he *is* Pelé!

CLOSE MARKING

I JOKINGLY SAY THAT until Juninho is 30 years old, I'll be on his back. I'll be watching him! Then, after he becomes a grown man, he can do whatever he wants. Even though he is a father now, increasingly mature and responsible, he is still my son.

Since he became a professional, Neymar Jr has always caught the attention of fans and, of course, of women. Besides preparing himself to be a great player, he has had to prepare himself for how to handle all the female attention. It wasn't easy then, and it's still not easy today. But the boy knows what to do.

I always have to be alert, but sometimes I just can't keep up. I used to tell him, 'Son, you must first achieve everything you have ever wanted and dreamed about as a footballer. Treat your career with the utmost importance. And then, later, you can enjoy your life in a more relaxed way. And you will enjoy it because you will have no regrets.' I think he learned this lesson well.

I've seen a lot and I know what it is like. In my time, when I was a player, the advances from the fans were not the same as they are today. Had he played in my time, Neymar Jr would still be a world-class player, but I believe the approach from fans would be different, especially from women.

But all this attention has a good side as well, especially with the younger fans. I remember that there was a boy with a brain tumour whose biggest dream was to meet Neymar Jr. My son visited him at the hospital, and the occasion was a great joy to everyone. Juninho even cried. Today, the boy has recovered. And the nice thing about that episode, besides his recovery, was that Neymar Jr didn't bother to make the story public. He didn't turn it into a publicity stunt. He did it because he wanted to and because he knew that he could bring some joy to another human being.

Like any parent, I also worry about alcohol and other substances. Fortunately I know that it's not in his nature to seek out forbidden experiences. He doesn't drink or take any illegal substances. He's a golden boy in that regard and I am very proud of him. He knows that, as a professional athlete, there are a lot of dos and don'ts.

Professional athletes often end up maturing faster than their peers both physically and emotionally. With Neymar Jr, that's no different. Everything with him came early, even fatherhood. But having children of your own is a great way to mature.

My own son and daughter are the most precious things to me in the world. The pride I have for Juninho and Rafaela is, I'm sure, the same that any parent has for their children. I'm very thankful for having such extraordinary and responsible kids.

The only thing I wish I had is more time to spend with my daughter. But, for now, this is a little tricky. It was a choice we had to make. Rafaela has been amazing at dealing with her brother's fame and success in a positive way. Even when she felt, 'Darn, my father is away with Juninho again,' she had the maturity to understand the situation and to make the best out of it. She is one of his greatest fans and she has been wonderful about dealing with living with a famous brother. She's a very special person. Nadine and I are blessed to have such great kids.

CONSOLIDATION AND LEARNING

MY FIRST GREAT CHALLENGE as a professional footballer came in 2009, in the first month of my career, at the Pacaembu Stadium, when we were playing against Corinthians in the Campeonato Paulista. The great Ronaldo, one of my idols, was playing for the opposing team. Ronaldo, the most prolific scorer in the history of the World Cup, had been my hero when growing up. I always tried to imitate him – his dribbles, his goals, and even his haircut from the 2002 World Cup. Seven years later, right after the national anthem, the man known as 'the phenomenon' came to talk to me. He hugged me and gave me a lot of encouragement, affection and respect. I was overwhelmed by his actions.

We didn't play very well that day and lost 1-0. We were able to recover later in the competition and made it to the play-offs after an incredible victory against Ponte Preta, scoring twice in the last eight minutes to beat them 3-2. Our confidence received a major boost from that result and we went on to eliminate Palmeiras in the next round. In the first game, at home, we won 2-1. I scored a beautiful goal that day. I received a pass from Roberto Brum in front of the penalty area and slid the ball between the goalie's legs to score.

That was a play I had learned from my father when I was ten years old. Inside the penalty area, with a defender in front of me, I learned to kick the ball through his legs. My father used to say, 'Move in front of him, and when he opens his legs, you pass the ball between them.' I'll never forget the first time it worked, when I was still playing for Portuguesa Santista. After the goal, I ran to the first row in the stand to thank my father for teaching me the technique.

The second game was a full-blooded affair, which featured a number of violent clashes, but we dealt with the onslaught well and won again, 2-1.

In the first leg of the two-game final we faced Corinthians at Vila Belmiro. Ronaldo was truly phenomenal and practically decided the result on his own. In the last game, at the Pacaembu, it was a one-all draw, which meant that Corinthians were Campeonato Paulista champions and Santos finished second. For a team that started the competition as an underdog written off by many from the outset, and for my first competitive season, it was a great experience.

Unfortunately, the rest of that year wasn't so good. We changed coaches and I was relegated back to the bench. Santos ended the Campeonato Brasileiro in 12th place. [The Campeonato Brasileiro is a nationwide league, like many major football leagues around the world, like the English Premier League, La Liga, the Bundesliga, or Serie A, consisting of 20 clubs who play each other home and away, to decide the Brazilian champion; there are four divisions, Série A to D, with promotion and relegation; Santos played in Série A.] I didn't play very often, but it wasn't just a matter of the coach's decision: I wasn't playing all that well – not badly, but not brilliantly either. Sometimes, that's how it goes. You have to be humble and very patient and just wait for your chance to come again.

2010 was a remarkable year for me, when I finally bedded myself into the Santos first team, one of the best teams I have ever played in. I was happy both on and off the pitch. The joy I felt playing and living with that group was amazing and we were able to use that good mood and close team bond to play some beautiful football.

We played with great joy, but at the same time with a great sense of responsibility. We were always having fun in training and also in the games. We had so much confidence running through that team. It's not that we were arrogant, but we knew that we needed to win, and this feeling was contagious. Of course, everything was easier with all the talent we had in the team.

The mood in the squad was great, but it got even better when one of my idols, Robinho, was brought back to Santos. When I saw him entering Vila Belmiro, being reintroduced to a full stadium, I couldn't believe my eyes. I thought, 'My God, my idol Robinho, playing alongside me! I used to watch him on the TV!' I never imagined playing with Robinho for Santos. I learned a lot from him and we soon created a really strong bond. It was just fantastic, one of the best years of my life. Because we were happy, we played happily and were able to bring so much joy to the fans and everyone who liked football.

We had a great defence: Rafael, our goalkeeper, Pará, Edu Dracena, Durval and Leo. They used to say to us up front, 'Don't worry, we'll take care of everything back here.' Arouca and Wesley were masters of the midfield, tirelessly running everywhere. Then up front, there was me, Ganso, Robinho and André. Ganso with his brilliant passes, me and Robinho dribbling past everyone, and André getting on the end of every rebound. I'm such a big fan of André's, because he positions himself so intelligently inside the penalty area. We used to start the play and, without looking, we just knew where he would be. When defences were tough to break down, we would often fire shots that missed, but André developed an incredible knack of always being there to score from the rebound.

That's how our team worked. It was really fun, even when I didn't play. There was a game against Ituano when Robinho and I were in the USA, and I asked my friends, 'If you score, remember me when you celebrate. I want you to imitate the Statue of Liberty.' Madson said, 'You got it.'

I was watching the game in New York and Santos went a goal down. I had to leave, so I didn't see the rest of the game. After a while, Ganso and André called me on my phone. They were in the middle of the post-game interviews, telling me that Madson had scored and had done the imitation. That was cool. They also told me we were live on television and I shouldn't say anything inappropriate. Then, they told me the news: the game had ended 9-1 to Santos! I was so pleased for them all.

The whole year was like that. We didn't always score as many goals as that, but we almost always won. We won the Campeonato

Paulista after two very hard games against Santo André. Then we won the Copa do Brasil, again after two real battles, this time against Vitória. In the first game, at Vila Belmiro, we won. But I missed a penalty kick: I tried a trick kick that had worked many times before. I thought, 'I'll kick down the middle, because the goalie always tries to jump to one side.' Since it was a final, I didn't think he would stay in the middle of the goal. But when I kicked, I immediately regretted it. The goalie didn't move and he saved it easily.

It was a hard moment, because everyone in the stadium started booing me. Every time I touched the ball, the crowd booed. Even our own fans. I thought to myself, 'Man, I have to do something, I have to help the team somehow.' And I had already scored once by this stage! We were winning, but it wasn't easy. We eventually won the competition, but right there, at Vila Belmiro, all I wanted was to compensate for my mistake. But I couldn't. It was one of the few times I was booed at home. In the middle of the finals! That hurt a lot. But I did learn a lesson.

Neymar preocupa o time do Paulista

A boa atuação do jogador no primeiro turno, quando o União venceu por 2 a 1, chamou a atenção

O atacante Neymar deve ser a maior atração do União/UMC contra o Paulista, domingo em Jundiaí. O jogador, que atuou pelo time jundiaiense na última temporada, é considerado pela Imprensa local o mais perigoso da equipe mogiana. No União, a maior preocupação é com o trabalho de bastidores do adversário. A diretoria já está tomando providências para evitar que a o alvirubro seja prejudicado.

A boa atuação de Neymar no jogo do primeiro turno, quando o União venceu o Paulista por 2 a 1, no Nogueirão, fez com que as atenções da imprensa de Jundiaí voltassem todas para o atacante. Por sua vez, o jogador demonstra não dar importância para este fato. "Estamos preocupados em fazer uma boa apresentação em Jundiaí e dar a vitória ao União", afirmou. Neymar espera casa cheia e um jogo difícil no domingo. "Eu conheço bem aquela cidade e sei que eles vão fazer de tudo para torcida comparecer", disse.

Neymar alertou quanto a dificuldade que o time mogiano terá em relação a arbitragem. "Lá não vai ser fácil, temos que ter cuidado para que não prejudiquem nosso time", afirmou. "Temos que achar um meio de neutralizar isto", completou. O técnico Paulo Comelli reforçou as palavras de Neymar. "Desde que assumi o União,

CONHECIDO - O atacante Neymar esteve emprestado pelo União/UMC a equipe jundiaiense na última temporada

nós fomos prejudicados em quase todos o jogos", reclamou Comelli. "Já alertei a diretoria sobre este problema e ela vai tomar providências", completou.

Em Jundiaí, o jogo está tomando dimensões de decisão. A diretoria do Paulista está promovendo várias atrações para promover a partida e estimular a ida dos torcedores. No intervalo da partida serão sorteados brindes e na entrada dos jogadores serão distribuídas camisetas. Até cheques pré-datados, para 30

dias, serão aceitos na compra de ingressos. O lateral-esquerdo Albéris, contundido, já é desfalque certo no time jundiaiense. O substituto imediato, Marquinhos, foi expulso no último jogo. Na posição entrará o jovem Pipoca, de 16 anos.

Neymar acidentado

Neymar, ponteiro direito da equipe profissional do União, sofreu um acidente automobilístico batendo seu Monza. Está sob observação médica. Possivelmente não jogará no próximo domingo, aqui, contra a Central Brasileira. Sua esposa e filho, que o acompanhavam na oportunidade, passam bem, tendo sofrido pequenas escoriações.

Neymar foi muito bem contra o Matonense, tendo sido o autor do tento de empate do alvirrubro. O jovem ponteiro vem agradando de jogo para jogo. Tem, inclusive, anotado tentos decisivos para a sua equipe. O moço, sem favor nenhum, tem sido no campeonato da Divisão Intermediária deste ano o melhor atacante unionista, com exibições regulares e sempre de alto nível. Esta coluna lamenta o acidente e espera que a recuperação desse excelente atleta seja a mais breve possível.

União 0 x Corinthians 0

Os cerca de sete mil torcedores que ontem foram assistir o amistoso entre SC Corinthians e União FC saíram do Estádio Cavalheiro Nami Jafet sem ver nenhum gol. Mas assistiram a um bom espetáculo. O atacante Viola, mesmo entrando no segundo tempo, foi o jogador mais aplaudido da noite. No entanto, o prêmio de melhor jogador ficou com o ponta direita Neymar, do União.

Snapshots from Neymar Sr's playing career, including a report on the car accident that left him bedridden for months and nearly claimed the life of his infant son.

Above left: Neymar Sr playing for Worker Lowland Grande.

Below left: Neymar Jr celebrating his first birthday with his mother, Nadine.

Above: Childhood memories, with Neymar Sr and sister, Rafaela.

Left and below:
Father and son,
always together.

Below left: Neymar Jr showing his delight at the safe arrival of his son, Davi Lucca.

Below right: With Davi Lucca before a training session at Santos.

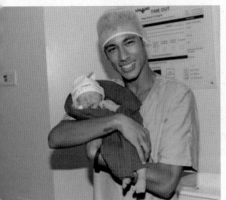

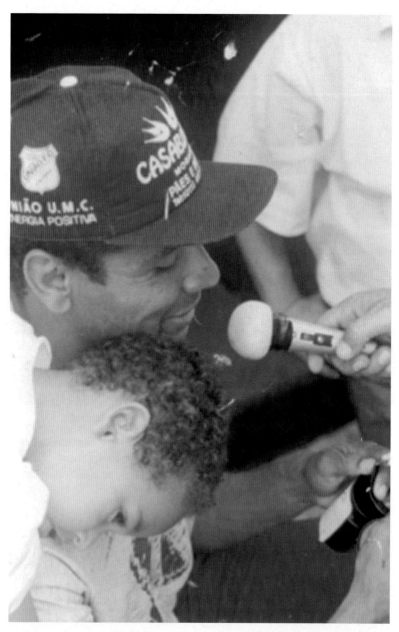

Father and son, inseparable, even when Neymar Sr is being interviewed during his playing heyday.

'I jokingly say that until Juninho is 30 years old, I'll be on his back. I'll be watching him!'

Neymar Jr's first club and Seleção membership cards.

Aged just seventeen, Neymar Jr celebrates after scoring against Rio Branco at Vila Belmiro in the Copa do Brasil on 18 March 2009. *Getty Images*

Neymar Jr and Robinho celebrate scoring against São Paulo at Vila Belmiro in the Campeonato Paulista on 18 April 2010. Robinho's return on loan from Manchester City was instrumental to Santos' success that season. *Getty Images*

André and Neymar Jr celebrate winning the Campeonato Paulista after defeating Santo André at the Pacaembu Stadium on 2 May 2010. *Getty Images*

Neymar Jr prepares to lift the 2011 Campeonato Paulista trophy after defeating Corinthians at Vila Belmiro. *Getty Images*

After Barcelona defeat Santos in the FIFA Club World Cup final, played in Yokohama on 18 December 2011, Lionel Messi (L) holds the Golden Ball trophy, midfielder Xavi (R) holds the Silver Ball trophy while Neymar Jr holds the Bronze Ball trophy. Just two years later, Juninho would be wearing the colours of the Catalan giants. *Getty Images*

Neymar Jr prepares to fire a goal-scoring strike into the back of the Guarani net during the first leg of the 2012 Campeonato Paulista final at Morumbi Stadium in São Paulo. Santos would win the game 3-0 and secure the title with a 4-2 second-leg victory. *Getty Images*

Neymar Jr celebrates scoring against São Paulo during the 2013 Campeonato Paulista. *Getty Images*

Juninho follows in the footsteps of Pelé, the King, by wearing Brazil's iconic number 10 shirt. *Getty Images*

Juninho at a photo shoot for Nike in 2013. *Getty Images*

Neymar Jr celebrates scoring the Seleção's opening goal during the 2013 Confederations Cup match against Japan at the National Stadium in Brasilia. *Getty Images*

Juninho rockets a shot past Iker Casillas of Spain to score in the final of the 2013 Confederations Cup as Brazil beat the World Cup and two-time European Cup holders 3-0. *Getty Images*

Posing with the Confederations Cup, the Golden Ball and Bronze Boot in the dressing room after the victory over Spain at the Maracanã. *Getty Images*

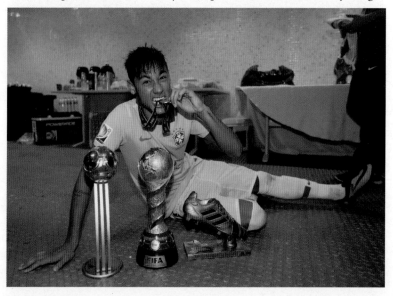

Running out for Barcelona at Camp Nou in 2013. *Getty Images*

Juninho is mobbed by his teammates after scoring the opening goal during the La Liga Clásico against Real Madrid at Camp Nou, 26 October 2013. *Getty Images*

Wheeling away in delight after scoring against Atlético Madrid in the
UEFA Champions League quarter-final first leg at Camp Nou on 1 April
2014. *Getty Images*

Juninho has never tried to hide or suppress the joy with which he plays
the game. *Getty Images*

Neymar Jr with his son, Davi Lucca, and Barcelona teammate, Lionel Messi (who holds his son, Thiago) before playing Real Sociedad in La Liga at the Camp Nou. *Getty Images*

MENINOS DA VILA 3.0

I WAS A RIGHT winger who relied more on my strength than my skills. Times were different back then, when there were a lot of refined footballers playing for the top club teams, who had a panache and beauty to their game. The difference on a technical level between a player at a major club and a player elsewhere seemed to be much bigger in those days. Those who played in the lower divisions had very little chance to progress to the elite teams; the skilful players had collected at the top of the pyramid, and if you played in a lower league or for a smaller club, you tended to play a more physical, less refined game. I think that is the reason I spent the majority of my career away from the big clubs. Today, the skill gap between players, and indeed clubs, is smaller. Maybe today I might have had a chance to make it to the top, because the style of play I'd have been able to play would have been different. But in those days, there was no way to get even close to a big club without a high skill level. Players like Aílton

Lira (from Santos) and Dicá (from Ponte Preta, but who also had a short spell at Santos) were actually quite slow, but with their skill level they completely bypassed that shortcoming.

In 1978, Aílton Lira and fellow veteran Clodoaldo formed a bedrock of experience in a great Santos team brimming with young talent, which included Pita and Juari, that became known as 'Meninos da Vila' after they became champions of the Campeonato Paulista.

In 2002, Robinho and Diego were part of the team that brought the glory days back to the club as they won the Campeonato Brasileiro. In the aftermath, the management invested a great deal of money in building new training facilities, which were named Meninos da Vila in tribute to the 1978 team; this moniker was then adopted again for the all-conquering 2010 team, which featured Neymar Jr, Ganso, André and the not so young, but eternally youthful, Robinho. Santos won the 2010 Campeonato Paulista and the Copa do Brasil. Robinho's skill and experience were indispensable that season and along with the wise management of Dorival Júnior and the youthful exuberance and skill of players like Neymar Jr and Paulo Henrique Ganso, it was a remarkable season.

That's when my son started to gain more maturity in his game and developed increasing tactical and spatial awareness, which allowed him to read the run of play better and better, which in turn allowed him to carve out more space for himself and his teammates and to create and finish more chances in front of goal. He also gained more weight, height and even started to grow a hint of a beard. He was still a boy who had just turned 18, but within that team he had the responsibilities of a grown man. The future seemed very bright.

The big turning point for Santos had been the return of Robinho to the club on loan from Manchester City in 2010. He was a leader for the young boys to follow, had vast experience gained at Real Madrid and in the English Premier League, and was a dependable rock to fall back on if things got tough both on and off the field.

We beat São Paulo 2-1 in his first game back, on 7 February. He came off the bench with 30 minutes to go and scored a beautiful goal against goalkeeper Rogério Ceni, who completely lost his temper during the match. It had all started when Neymar Jr scored a penalty using the Brazilian *paradinha*, a feint in which the player stops unexpectedly during his run. Ceni – a fantastic goalie, who is himself an expert at taking penalty and free kicks – was infuriated by the way Juninho took the penalty. I didn't really understand why, since it was technically perfectly legitimate; penalties are about mind games as much as they are about technical execution. But I guess Ceni didn't appreciate being made to look a bit of a fool when he reacted early, diving to one side and allowing Juninho to slot home in a virtually open goal.

Juninho was fantastic in the Campeonato Paulista, and scored in every match. He missed a penalty against Corinthians, at home, but he scored a beautiful goal right after, and Santos won the match 2-1. There was another uncomfortable moment in that game, when Neymar Jr passed the ball over the head of defender Chicão, after the referee had blown his whistle; it was really just a little trick, showing how much fun he was having, but there was a bad reaction to it in the media with people accusing him of being conceited and smug. He was just having some fun, like many athletes do, but that's how it sometimes goes in football. When you're winning, it's all fun. When you lose, everything becomes criticism and controversy. That goes for everyone. There are no saints in football.

In the semi-finals, Santos recorded two big victories over São Paulo. We won the first match 3-2 at the Morumbi Stadium. Having been ahead 2-0 in the first half, we let them back in the game to tie things 2-2, but Durval scored in the last minutes to secure victory. In the second leg, we won 3-0, and Juninho scored the second goal, again with a penalty, and again with the *paradinha* against Rogério Ceni. That goal paved the way to another final. And it was very nice to hear the fans pleading for Juninho to be called up to the Seleção.

To be fair, the entire team was playing very well: Robinho, André, Marquinhos, Arouca, Wesley, and especially Ganso. Many people were clamoring for Dunga, then coach of the Seleção, to take Neymar Jr and Ganso to the 2010 World Cup in South Africa. It certainly was a dream of ours that Juninho might one day represent Brazil on the world stage. We knew it would take hard work to make those dreams come true, but we also knew that becoming champions of the Campeonato Paulista would help his cause.

Both legs of the final, against Santo André, were played at the Pacaembu Stadium. They went ahead early in the first match, but we rallied to win 3-2, thanks largely to a great performance from André. Juninho was replaced at half-time because he had a problem with his eyes. He did not play very well, and neither did the team, even though they won.

In the final match, we had the advantage and we knew it would be a very tough game. But it ended up being even harder than we had expected. Santo André scored after only 25 seconds.

Neymar Jr tied the score seven minutes later, and would score again in the end of the first half, but we ultimately lost the game, 3-2. Tied 5-5 on aggregate, we became champions because we had come first in the league table, just ahead of Santo André, before the knock-out stages.

As a Santos fan, I was delighted, of course. But because my son had been part of the team, I must say that I struggle to articulate quite how I was really feeling. I was very emotional when I saw Juninho receiving the gold medal and parading through the stadium wearing the jersey that once belonged to Pelé, Pepe, Zito, Clodoaldo, Carlos Alberto Torres, Pita, Juari, Serginho Chulapa, Paulo Isidoro, Robinho, Diego, among many other greats that gone before him at Vila Belmiro, Pacaembu, Morumbi, Maracanã, and so many other stadiums throughout the world.

Now, my son was part of the club's victorious history. And better yet, it was the first of many victories. I was certain that many more would come. We had worked hard to get to that point, but I honestly hadn't expected so much, so soon. He was named in the team of the year and as player of the season.

The Campeonato Paulista title gave a great boost to the confidence of the team, but I can't hide the fact that I was saddened when Juninho didn't make the cut for the 2010 World Cup. I understand that Dunga, the coach, already had the team he wanted, and that's very important in football. Our disappointment was tempered by the fact that, at the time, even Pelé and Zico were publicly voicing their support for Neymar Jr and Ganso to be selected for the Seleção. Messi himself thought the absence of the boys was odd. But there wasn't much that could be done about it, so we respected Dunga's decision.

After the sorrow of losing the World Cup quarter-final, Santos' fans had some joy soon after when the team won the Copa do Brasil. Santos deserved to win that competition after the extraordinary number of goals they scored. At Vila Belmiro, in the very first game, Santos beat Naviraiense 10-0. Juninho scored twice. Then the team beat Remo 4-0. Again, he scored two. In the next game, more impressive numbers: 8-1 against Guarani, at Vila Belmiro. It was one of Juninho's best matches. He scored five times! It felt like the good old days, when Pelé played for Santos. Except that it was now the Santos of Neymar Jr and his friends.

In the quarter-finals, after a 3-2 first-leg defeat to Atlético Mineiro, Santos had a great victory at home, 3-1, with another goal by Neymar Jr, to progress to the next round. In the semi-finals, they faced another tough match. We were defeated 4-3 away from home by Grêmio. However, in the second match, the team responded brilliantly and won 3-1, making it to the finals.

In the first leg, against Vitória at Vila Belmiro, Santos won 2-0. Neymar Jr missed a penalty, but scored a goal from open play. It's a shame that the missed penalty seemed more important than the goal for many people. He tried a trick kick in the middle of the goal, but the goalkeeper guessed his strategy and saved the shot easily. The coach summed it up well after the match: 'If he had scored, they would say he is daring, but since he missed, they say now that he is irresponsible.'

In the last match, away from home at the Barradão Stadium, captain Edu Dracena scored a beautiful header and Santos won the only title that the club had never previously held: they were champions of the Copa do Brasil! It was the crowning moment for a very young, yet superb, team. That title gave everyone the feeling that Brazilian football could soon regain its majesty of days past. It just needed to make the right choices – with selection, management, tactics and long-term strategy.

They were a team with a wonderful balance between the attacking élan of players like Neymar Jr, Ganso, Robinho, Marquinhos, André, Arouca, and Wesley, and the rock-solid defence behind them. They scored 130 goals that season.

Still, there were many people who tried to find fault with the team and my son, saying they made too many unnecessary plays and Juninho took too many dives. I never saw it that way. What I saw was that the team, and Neymar Jr, were on the road to even bigger achievements than the Campeonato Paulista and the Copa do Brasil.

That year was an incredibly emotional ride for me as a father, a fan and a former player. Neymar Jr comes from the stands at the stadium. He comes from the club's youth divisions. And he is his father's son: he is fanatical about Santos FC. He may now have left Santos, but Santos will never leave him. It's the place where he was born – both figuratively and literally. Vila Belmiro is our home.

I'LL STAY

I REMEMBER LIKE IT was yesterday. It was 23 August 2010. My father and I had a meeting with president Luis Álvaro at the Santos headquarters inside Vila Belmiro. Chelsea had made a huge offer for me.

In the middle of our conversation, the president turned off the lights and pointed at an empty chair. 'This chair belong to the nation's greatest sporting hero. Since Ayrton Senna's death, this chair has sat vacant. If Neymar Jr turns down Chelsea's offer and stays at Santos, he will have taken his first step towards sitting there.'

That made us think. How could it not? It was the start of the 'Neymar Project', an innovative idea that even won a few marketing awards. It was my father's idea; he wanted to find a way not just to fund my staying, but also to help my family and my projects beyond football. There had never been anything like it to keep a player in the country, and it ended up being good for everyone, not just because of what we earned, but for all that we helped to bring to Santos and to Brazilian football.

Everyone was very tense at that meeting, because it was my future on that table. That decision would be a turning point in my life, whichever way it turned out. Pelé even called me. Can you imagine how important I felt? The King called and asked me to stay. He reminded me that he had spent his entire competitive career with Santos, he had won major trophies with the club and he had established his legend with the Seleção while playing for Santos. Of course, it was a different time, a different world, a different football. We considered all of that as we pondered our final decision. But after a short time, I had no doubt whatsoever: we would turn down the offer, just as we had with Real Madrid in 2006.

It wasn't easy. But, as before, it was the right decision for us. We did the right thing for our family, friends and my career. We helped to solidify, even more, our roots at Vila Belmiro, bringing more money to Santos and helping to recover the esteem of Brazilian football. I'm happy I was part of all of that with my father and the managers at Santos. Again, we thought more about my happiness and development as an athlete than we thought about money. I don't sell myself for money. Of course, money is a big help, but my life and my career are not governed by it. I have my feet on the ground, and my head is in the right place. That's why we decided to stay with Santos in 2010.

Afterwards, in the Campeonato Brasileiro, I admit we didn't do so well. Robinho had to return to Europe to play for his new club, AC Milan, and we ended the competition in 8th place. Nevertheless, I scored 16 times and was runner-up for top striker. But for many people, that competition will be remembered for my argument with our coach, Dorival Júnior, at a match against Atlético Goianiense, in Vila Belmiro.

We were winning 3-2 when the referee awarded us a penalty. I had been training and performing as our lead penalty taker, even though I had missed a few. But out of the blue, the coach asked Marcel to do it. Things got pretty heated and Edu Dracena, our captain, also weighed in. It got ugly, but it was all part of the game. In the dressing room afterwards, things were still tense. I raised my voice, and so did he. But we made peace right there and then. He called me to his office, said everything he had to say and we resolved our differences. It was all good, but then his assistant restarted the argument. So, tensions rose again. In the end, I received a punishment. The managers wanted to give me a one-game ban but the coach wanted more. They had a disagreement of their own, and Dorival ended up being fired.

I don't like controversy. When I get myself into these situations, it's usually because of something I've done on the pitch, rather than something I have said or done off it. I would never work against a professional, especially someone in a higher position. I obey the orders I receive, that's how I have achieved everything I have. However, in the heat of the game, I have to admit that sometimes I lose it.

I was very sorry about the whole ordeal and the departure of a coach who had helped me so much. I don't hold any grudges, and I know that he also doesn't. As a matter of fact, when we met again in November of that year, in a match between Santos and his new team, Atlético Mineiro, we shared a friendly hug. Dorival is a great person.

In life and in football, we are here to make friends, not enemies, even with those at rival clubs – like Paulinho, who was a defender for Corinthians and is my colleague in the Seleção. We're great friends and he used to play for our biggest rival. So what?

In the episode with Dorival Júnior, there was no real problem. But people kept seeing what was not there and making up theories of things that never happened. That's another side of fame, another obstacle I have to learn how to overcome, yet one that I hadn't ever practiced in all the hours of preparing myself for this career as a child.

I know I was very wrong on that occasion. It was one of the worst days of my life. That was not me. I knew afterwards that I needed to become a better man, I needed to mature. But I did learn my lesson, as a person and as a professional. With that penalty, all I wanted was to help the team. I wasn't being individualistic. I had a fight not only with my coach, but also with my captain. I felt horrible when I heard about Dorival being fired. I thought it was all my fault, and even though everyone was telling me that it was not, I still felt guilty, especially because Dorival Júnior is such a good person and such a fine coach.

I never cried like I did that day. I was devastated. I remember my father was ill. I left the club and went home. He and my mother were also crying. She had been crying since the game, when she saw me in that situation. She said that was not her son. Not the Juninho she knew and loved. I'll never forget that. I felt even worse when I heard her saying that. However, it also helped me to grow up and never make the same mistake again.

In the following days, turning on the TV was hard. Everyone was criticising me; I was called a monster. Those were horrible nights. I kept asking God for forgiveness hour after hour, minute after minute. If it hadn't been for my friends and my family, I wouldn't be where I am today. I was so close to quitting football altogether.

My friends, once more, were my partners. They gave me support and helped me, just like my family. I didn't want to leave the house, and they stayed with me. My friends are very loyal, like real brothers. A bakery next to my house hung a sign harshly criticising me. My friends wanted to tear down the sign, but I said that they shouldn't, because the fans have the right to always say what they are thinking.

I got through the pain with the love of my dearest ones and by learning from my mistake. You can never justify a mistake. My parents always taught me to not try to explain my mistakes, but try to learn from them. In my darkest hours, my family will always be by my side. They are my most loyal fans, and my most important team.

2011

I T WAS MARCH, 2011. The second leg of the Campeonato
Paulista final. In the 38th minute of the second half, Juninho
kicked the ball from the left. The Corinthians goalkeeper,
Júlio César, couldn't hold it, and the ball slowly crossed the line.
It felt like a movie. Actually, better than that: it was like a trilogy,
and that was only the second of the three Campeonato Paulista
titles Juninho would win.

Coach Adílson Batista, who had replaced Dorival Júnior,
had already left the club – just a few months after taking
up the reins. Juninho was not long back from playing with
the under-20 Brazilian national team, who had won the
Campeonato Sudamericano Sub-20 [the South American
Under-20 Cup] in Peru, and he barely had any time to work
with Batista before he was on his way out. These things happen
in Brazilian football.

It was not an easy win for Santos. Ganso had missed a lot of the season while recovering from knee surgery. He played only eight matches in the Campeonato Paulista that year. But even if he had played just one it would have been enough to notice the difference that he could make to a team. He was an exceptional player.

Robinho wasn't with Santos anymore, so the management brought back another great champion from that team of 2002-04. Elano arrived from Europe, where he had been playing for Galatasaray, and joined the squad as if he had never left Vila Belmiro. He was playing very well and helped a lot with his experience. As Robinho had done, he acted like a big brother for the rest of the team.

In the first six rounds of the Campeonato Paulista, Juninho was away playing for the Brazilian under-20 team, and Ganso was recuperating from injury. We were at the top of the table, having won four matches and tied another two, scoring an average of three goals per match. However, things went downhill from there. We only won three of the next six matches. Then, our first match in the Copa Libertadores da América ended with a tie and coach Adílson Batista left, never having had the entire team at his command. The assistant coach, Marcelo Martelotte, assumed the position and did well: with him, Santos won six matches, tied one and lost only three until the arrival of coach Muricy Ramalho.

Ganso was already on his way to a full recovery. Muricy then put Danilo in the midfield to protect our defence, finding a way to suffocate our opponents' attacking play. It wasn't until the quarter-finals of the Campeonato Paulista that we had all of our main players back in harness together, and with them in place we went on to beat Ponte Preta.

In the semi-final, decided by a single knockout game rather than over two legs, we faced a São Paulo side that was on a roll and felt that they had the momentum and quality to beat us at the Morumbi Stadium. But in a very fortunate afternoon for all Santos fans – and especially for my son and Ganso – we secured a great 2-0 victory.

So, we were through to our third consecutive Campeonato Paulista final. The problem was that Santos was competing on two fronts at the time, playing in both the Libertadores da América and Campeonato Paulista. Ganso didn't even finish the first half of the first leg of the Campeonato Paulista final at the Pacaembu Stadium, against our rival Corinthians. It ended 0-0, although the goalpost didn't help much, for Neymar Jr almost scored with two great strikes that both just clipped the woodwork to go wide.

The next day, a newspaper ran the headline, 'Neymar vs the rest'. It wasn't exactly the case, but admittedly, it felt a little like it. The paper counted at least seven great plays from my son: hitting the post twice, various dribbles, crosses and passes, etc. On that day, he really played very well. Played like a veteran, even though he was still so young.

However, the entire team played even better in the final, at home. Winning the championship at our own stadium was unforgettable. Neymar Jr scored the last goal and we all celebrated a record: no other club had won so many consecutive Campeonato Paulista titles. It was the sixth time that Santos had won it two times in a row. Winning a competition is not easy. Winning it twice is even harder. But then we turned our thoughts to winning the Libertadores da América for a third time . . . Now that would be a challenge.

What a thrill as a fan and a father! I didn't see Santos win the Libertadores in 1962, against Peñarol. I also didn't see the second win, in 1963, with the legendary team led by Pelé, against Boca Juniors. But now, I could say it out loud: I saw my team win the Libertadores da América! I saw my son celebrating on the pitch with the squad that was so well led by coach Muricy Ramalho.

The Copa Libertadores da América is one of the most highly-regarded tournaments in the world and the most prestigious club competition in South American football. It is the equivalent of the Champions League in South American football.

There is a very beautiful image from this historic game that you can now see in the official film of the club's centenary. All the players are celebrating together, the fans are singing in unison, and Juninho is kneeling with his arms outstretched to the heavens. It was beautiful to see that white ocean of Santos shirts filling the Pacaembu Stadium. Santos, three-time champions of the Libertadores da América. Amazing.

It was a magnificent campaign and an incredible last match against Peñarol. The first leg of the final had been a bruising encounter in Uruguay and it had been hard to watch because the Peñarol defence tackled my son very hard. They had a good team and an amazing history. But we had more than that, and we played better. We drew the first leg 0-0 and won the second 2-1. It was Santos' first Libertadores since the Pelé era. And seeing Pelé himself on the pitch celebrating like he had also won the title was a magical moment.

Some of the Santos players were heavily criticised during the campaign, much of which I felt was unfair. For example, Zé Love was very important to Muricy Ramalho's tactical approach and he helped his teammates a lot, but he was often misunderstood by the fans and the press. But what I saw out there was a warrior. He overcame everything, including the media furore, and was crucial for the success of the team.

You can't win an international title relying on the talent of just some key players. You need a strong group with a number of options for the coach, and also a good structure from the coaching staff. All of that was provided by the managers, and the club won an historic title.

From a personal point of view, it was magnificent that our victory was decided by my son: Arouca carried the ball from the midfield and found him out on the left wing. He passed to Neymar Jr, who only had time for one touch before he was closed down by a defender. But with that one touch, Juninho had buried the ball in the net. The match had been fiercely close to that point, but we created a lot more opportunities than they did. Maybe we had 15, 17 chances to score. In the heat of the game, it's hard to tell.

The emotions after a goal are always indescribable. But, seeing your 19-year-old son scoring the goal that wins a title that the club hasn't won for 48 years really is too difficult to put into words. I can only imagine what was going through Juninho's mind at that time. I sincerely can't remember how I celebrated at the stadium. There were thousands of hearts beating in unison. And my heart was almost coming out of my chest. Honestly, I can't describe it. It was too much for me and always will be. I know other titles will come, but that one, with Juninho and the rest of the team playing like that for Santos, will always be special.

That first goal of the match paved our way to victory. And

then, to the delight of the fans, it was 2-0! The goal was scored by Danilo, in jersey number 22, 23 minutes into the second half. On that day, 22 June 2011, the team weren't just 11 white jerseys on the pitch, they were the entire group of 22. The entire club were playing together, fighting together. There's no way around it: to become champion you need to be united, both on the pitch and in the stands, all as one team: one champion.

But Peñarol were tough. They managed to claw a goal back and were on the attack for the rest of the game, chasing the equaliser. On paper, the final score was close, but I feel that Peñarol were lucky in many ways because we missed a lot of counterattacking opportunities. It could have been a lot more than 2-1. But the title was ours. We showed that it's possible to become champions using skill alone, without succumbing to the antagonistic violence and physicality that some teams tried to bully us with. We won the same way that Pelé did with his great team, by playing football. By never running away. We won on the pitch, with a lot of soul and suffering.

I didn't see Peñarol's goal. I was coming down to the dressing rooms and only heard the screams from the Uruguayan crowd. I had the torment of watching the final minutes on a small TV in a room nearby. I could hardly see anything, but then celebrated like there was no tomorrow when the referee blew for full time.

It was an epic victory that we'll celebrate forever – and it seemed to take forever to find Juninho afterwards. It took almost 40 minutes for them to raise the cup, and then there was the typical mayhem in the dressing rooms, with celebrations, interviews, and so on. After an eternity, I finally hugged my son. But, as always, after congratulating him, I pointed out to him a few missed opportunities and he also talked about some bad plays. That's how we are, we just can't help it.

And I'll take another 48 years without winning a competition just to remember the joy that he and Santos gave me that day.

It is such a pity that, after Santos won the Campeonato Paulista and the Libertadores da América, Brazil couldn't win the Copa América, the South American international championship. I wasn't upset by our elimination or my son's performance. Yes, I was frustrated, but what mattered was that he gained more experience. We can learn a lot from our defeats.

My son had always dreamed of playing for the national team. When he was called up for the first time, for coach Mano Menezes' debut game, against the USA in August 2010, his dream finally became a reality. But in the first game of the 2011 Copa América against Venezuela, things didn't go the way we wanted. Brazil didn't play well. The team was made up primarily of players from Santos: Robinho, Ganso and Neymar Jr. The midfield was the same line-up that had shone the previous year. But they seemed nervous in that first game. Juninho played well in the first half, and Brazil had a few chances to score, but in the second half everything went downhill, and the match ended 0-0.

We had an opportunity to make up for things against Paraguay, but Brazil played even worse. It ended in another tie, 2-2, and Juninho was booed at the end, and he preferred not to talk to the press. Robinho was replaced by Jadson, and he scored a beautiful goal in the first half. However, once again, things got worse in the second half. My son missed a shot, and when things don't work, everyone comes at you.

Paraguay took the lead 22 minutes into the second half. Coach Mano Menezes replaced Ramires with Lucas, to try and inject some more speed into the team and then replaced Neymar Jr with striker Fred – and it was he who scored to tie again at the very end.

The replacements were effective, but not enough. We needed to win the third match, and I had many things to talk about with my son. He had been booed before when playing for Santos, but when playing for Brazil it's a different thing entirely. There are fans from all teams, and some straight-up dislike Santos and Neymar Jr, so they don't hold back.

In the third match, feeling more relaxed and confident, Juninho and the entire team started to play better. Robinho was brought back, and he and Neymar Jr were a very effective partnership against Ecuador. Alexandre Pato scored the first goal to give Brazil the lead, but Ecuador tied the match shortly afterwards. In the second half, we finally played to our potential. Within four minutes, Neymar Jr had scored after a great pass from Ganso. Ten minutes later, Ecuador tied again, but we regained the lead once more after only two minutes, through Pato. As things stood, we were in first place in our group.

But there was more drama to come: Maicon crossed from the right and Juninho scored his second goal. Then, he made a hand gesture to his ears, provoking the crowd. The booing in the previous match had upset him. After all, people have feelings. He was then replaced and the entire stadium applauded. Juninho knows when he plays well and when he doesn't.

The victory ensured passage to the quarter-finals, where we met Paraguay again. I think that was our best match, but we missed a number of scoring opportunities. Juninho could have scored after only three minutes, but he messed up his connection with the ball. He had another opportunity later, but again he missed. In the first half, our defence was perfect and we played a lot better than Paraguay, but we didn't score. In the second half, it was the same story: their defender saved a goal from my son right at the start, and their goalie was inspired that day. He saved a series of great shots. On the other hand, our goalie practically didn't touch the ball. We must have had ten opportunities to score, against none from them.

With 34 minutes gone in the second half, the coach decided to replace Neymar Jr with Fred. Nobody likes to be replaced, and I think he could have stayed on. It was the best match Brazil had played in the Copa América, and one of the best that year. However, sometimes things go wrong. In extra time, we had a couple more chances to score, but again we didn't. And then, in the penalty shootouts, our horrible day was completed. We missed our four penalty kicks. It really wasn't our day.

My son was distraught. He knew he could've done better. But that's life. After our best performance of the tournament, we missed four penalty kicks. That's not normal. It had never happened with the Seleção before. But what's done is done.

Right after the elimination from the Copa América, something wonderful happened to my son. Though he hadn't made history with the Seleção in 2011, he would achieve an unprecedented feat for Santos right afterwards.

There were exactly a thousand days left until the 2014 World Cup. And maybe we'll need a thousand more days until another match like this happens: Santos vs. Flamengo, at Vila Belmiro, for the Campeonato Brasileiro. Our team was going through a purple patch and so was Neymar Jr. Flamengo, meanwhile, had a star of their own: Ronaldinho Gaúcho.

It was probably the best match Juninho ever played for Santos. And probably also the best match Ronaldinho ever played with Flamengo. The final score says everything you need to know: 5-4. We got a lead of 3-0 after only 30 minutes. Santos were playing very well, but so were Flamengo. Santos deserved the three goals, but Flamengo deserved more than that. They created and missed some incredible opportunities. It could easily have been 3-2 at that stage.

Ronaldinho and Neymar Jr were both incredible that day. My son scored the most beautiful goal of his career so far. That goal was awarded the Puskás Award by FIFA, an award to the 'most aesthetically significant goal of the year.' Puskás was a Hungarian star who had played for Real Madrid in the 50s and 60s. He was a guy who knew how to build plays and score amazing goals.

Juninho described the goal to a TV show this way:

Their right winger, Léo Moura, was behind me, and their defender, Williams, was coming towards me. I had to pass through the middle of them. Then I dribbled the ball and did just that. Then I saw our striker, Borges. I always exchange quick passes with him. He is a very skilful and intelligent player, he thinks very fast. I passed the ball and Borges passed back. Then I carried the ball and Renato came to me, so I protected it. In that moment, at that speed, I thought I would have to go past defender Ronaldo Angelim, and the first thing that came to my mind (and my feet) is that I would have to make a *meia-lua* manoeuvre: that's a trick when you kick the ball to one side and run to the other side. And it worked. When the goalie came to me, I just passed the ball over him and ran to celebrate.

Speaking like that, it doesn't seem so hard, and it doesn't seem that beautiful. However, with some plays, the player doesn't have much time to think. He touches the ball, passes, dribbles past his opponents and scores, all without thinking. It's a matter of skill, not strength. Facing all that adrenalin, the player must be agile and serene. You can't go crazy when the opportunity to score comes. You have to trust your instincts. Look at the goalie, the defenders, and think very fast. It's hard to explain. You just go and do it. If it works, that's great. If it doesn't, well, try again and again.

That was a match we will never forget, like many in Santos' history. Juninho was even awarded a plaque at the stadium, the same way that Pelé was after his famous *gol de placa* against Fluminense in 1961, at the Maracanã. There was another great match in the 1958 Rio-São Paulo Torneio [tournament], at the Pacaembu Stadium. It pitched Santos against Palmeiras, which Santos won 7-6, a hugely impressive spectacle worthy of a place in history, comparable to classic matches between Santos and Flamengo, of Pelé vs. Zico, of Neymar Jr vs. Ronaldinho. In this instance, with this match, there is no need for false modesty. It really was up there with the very best.

Although we lost that game, we can say that the biggest winner was football itself. Both teams deserved the three points awarded to the winner. Or maybe the winner deserved six points, for it was truly something remarkable.

A FOOTBALL LESSON

IT WAS A FOOTBALL lesson. Santos lost the FIFA Club World Cup not just to the champions of Europe in 2011, but to one of the best teams of all time. While we did create a few opportunities in the final match, we barely saw the ball, as with all teams who faced that magnificent Barcelona team. We knew it would be difficult. The whole world knew Barcelona were ahead of us, but we were well prepared. We were neither too confident nor too afraid of their team.

We tried to play. We tried to do the same thing we did when we won the Libertadores. But we weren't successful. Messi, Iniesta, Xavi and the others were just too inspired, too good. They were like players from another planet. They marked us very well and they knew what to do with the ball when they had it. On the other hand, we didn't play half as well as we could have, and that settled the result. To me, despite the defeat, it was a great life and football lesson. I learned a lot from that match.

We'd had a good win in the first game of the competition. We beat Kashiwa Reysol, 3-1. I scored with my left foot from quite a long way out. I'd never scored a goal from such a distance with my left foot before, and I did it in the World Championship.

Santos didn't win that competition, but someday we will. And between you and me, after what the Seleção did to Spain in the final match of the 2013 Confederations Cup, we can say that history can be rewritten in each match.

Today, I play for Barcelona with the same passion, dedication and affection that I gave to the glorious jersey of Santos. I expect to learn in Spain a lot more than I did in those 90 minutes of the final match of the Club World Cup.

On that day, I received both affection and respect from the legendary Messi. Besides his genius on the field, his modesty is admirable. He has won so much, yet still keeps the same modesty and simplicity. He is a great example. I hope to help him win even more titles as I play alongside him. Though, of course, I hope he doesn't win anything else when playing against me. After all, he also plays for Argentina, while I play for Brazil.

CAMPEONATO PAULISTA
2012

NEYMAR JR IS ALWAYS seeking the ball. He's not interested in resting. His joy is the ball. It's the game. It's being on the pitch. The coaches often want to give him a rest because of the crazy marathon of matches and training that they face during the course of a season, but he doesn't want to know. He wants to get on the pitch and give all he can, everywhere. He's a really dedicated athlete, who loves to play and train.

The physical wear and tear expected from a season like 2011, which was virtually without rest, didn't stop him from playing at an equally high level in 2012. His desire to win also helped him overcome problems and, with his teammates, win a third Campeonato Paulista in a row.

In November 2011, we reached a new deal, and Juninho stayed in Brazil. It was quite an accomplishment for him, Santos, and for all Brazilian football: it was a statement to the rest of the world, saying that Brazil had the means to keep an athlete like

Juninho. And he did well in the Campeonato Paulista, in Santos FC's centenary year. Also during that season, at just 20 years old, he scored his 100th goal in the derby match against Palmeiras.

In the semi-final against São Paulo, he scored a hat-trick in our 3-1 victory. In that year, Neymar Jr surpassed the records of every top striker at the club since the Pelé era. Each time that happened, he paid homage, imitating the gestures of those who had gone before him. Against São Paulo, he imitated Juari in the Meninos da Vila of 1978, when he circled the corner post each time he scored. Then, in the final against Guarani, at the Morumbi Stadium, he collapsed to the ground just like Serginho Chulapa did when he scored the winning goal in 1984. Juninho's goal in that first-leg match practically settled the third consecutive title for Santos, which was confirmed on the next Sunday when we beat Guarani, 4-2.

At the end of the match, 30 minutes after winning the title, Juninho started to dribble the ball around photographers and TV reporters on the pitch, with the fans shouting 'Olé!' Some said afterwards that it was a publicity stunt, but that's not right. He did it in the heat of the moment. He started to dribble around the press, and the whole stadium started to laugh. It was an amazing sight. It was neither snobbish nor teasing. It was just a boy doing his thing, his art – a somewhat mischievous kind of art, but art nevertheless.

We had won our third Campeonato Paulista. Now, it was time to fight for our second Libertadores da América. We lost the first match of the semi-final, playing at home, to Corinthians, 1-0. In the second leg, at the Pacaembu Stadium, Santos scored first, with a goal from my son, but Corinthians tied the match at the start of the second half, and the team never fully recovered from that blow. Well, that happens. You can't always win.

THE NATIONAL TEAM

I WANT TO WIN the World Cup for the people of my country. I also want to bring home a gold medal from the Olympic Games. I wish I had played the 2011 U-20 World Cup, but I was playing for the senior team in the Copa América, so I missed that great win for the under-20s, who had been led brilliantly by coach Ney Franco.

I played in the U-17 World Cup and our team didn't do so well, so it was disappointing to miss out on the under-20 triumph. That's why I dream about victory in the 2014 World Cup and 2016 Olympic Games. Then, I want to play in the 2018 and 2022 World Cups. I'll try, with the help of my teammates, to win everything I can. I want more victories, for the Seleção and for my club.

Every athlete wants to win but, of course, we can't win everything. In every game you play you face players also trying their best to win and to fulfil their own lifelong ambitions and dreams. As much as you try, sometimes things go wrong. There are things that are beyond our control. That's why we always have to be physically and mentally prepared to the best of our ability, because when it's your turn, you have to give all you can. And you may never get another chance.

That's what I have tried to do since ever since I was first called up to the Seleção, in August 2010. It was, as my father has written here previously, coach Mano Menezes' first game in charge after replacing Dunga after the World Cup, where the Seleção had been eliminated in the quarter-finals in South Africa by Holland. I suffered a lot that day watching the game. First and foremost I am a fan and I always want the best for Brazil.

I'll never forget that match of 10 August 2010 – a friendly against the USA, in New Jersey. We won 2-0 and I scored my first international goal. Though every game I play for Brazil is a huge thing for me, the first time was particularly special. I cried uncontrollably after losing the gold medal match to Mexico at the London 2012 Olympics. I feel it's a debt I owe to myself and my country. I still intend to settle it. If I have another chance, I'll turn those tears of pain into tears of joy. And, God help me, it will be at home, in 2014 and 2016, at our beloved Maracanã. All I want is a chance to scream 'Campeão' with Brazil.

SILVER DREAM

DURING THE PREPARATIONS FOR the 2012 London Olympics, I called Juninho and told him to do what he does best: to play to the best of his abilities, with his usual sense of responsibility, but also with his usual sense of joy. He was in London making another of his childhood dreams come true: to participate in the Olympic Games and compete for a gold medal. We took our usual bet – I always enjoyed betting with him, as a way to give even more encouragement. However, this time I was the one who won the bet. He didn't get the present I usually give him, because he lost the final.

In the first game against Egypt, Brazil won 3-2. Neymar Jr played well and scored one of the goals, but the second half made me worry, because the team's performance worsened. Since it was the first match, I put it down to the pressure. After all, it was an under-23 team. Even with three players allowed in each team over this age limit, the group was still rather young and had to carry the weight of Brazil having never won a football Olympic gold.

The match against Belarus was a showpiece for Neymar Jr to display his wares to the rest of the world. He made the pass that created Brazil's first goal. Then he scored with a free kick and gave another pass for the third goal. Against New Zealand, Brazil had already qualified for the next round, but none of the main players were rested. The team was more relaxed and, although they didn't play brilliantly, they won 3-0.

In the quarter-final against Honduras, I feared the worst, but Neymar Jr again played well, in a much improved team performance. After falling behind to an early goal, Juninho started the play that ended in the equaliser. Honduras took the lead again, but Brazil was awarded a penalty soon after. Despite the booing against the referee's decision, Neymar Jr coolly slotted home. In the end, Leandro Damião scored the decisive goal and Brazil won a very tough match, 3-2.

Despite their struggles, Brazil were through to the semi-finals and would have an opportunity to play in two medal-winning matches (either in the final, to contest gold and silver, or in a play-off with the other losing semi-finalist for bronze). Despite this lifting some of the tension in the camp, there was still a feeling that, without the gold, the campaign would be considered a failure. In Brazil, silver medals have a bitter taste.

The semi-final against South Korea was much easier than we had anticipated. I enjoyed the way Juninho played that day. He didn't score, but he played a critical role in the victory. He traded passes with Oscar for the first goal, crossed the ball for the second, and after the third goal, he was stepped up to become maestro in the team, controlling the rhythm until the end. The last time Brazil played an Olympic final was in 1988. And in those 24 years, there had been a lot of great teams that failed to go that far.

On the day of the big game, I was very nervous. I knew what it meant to Neymar Jr and the new generation of players like Lucas, Oscar and Pato. They all got along very well away from the game and so the spirit in the camp was strong, and talking with Juninho on the phone, I could sense their eagerness to win gold.

In football, you never know what might have happened if something had gone differently at some point in the game. But the goal that Mexico scored right at the start of the match had a destabilizing effect our team. Throughout the match, Neymar Jr was very well marked and started to get irritated by his lack of chances. As much as we had talked previously about what to do in such situations, you can't always correct it in the heat of the game like that, in an Olympic final, when everyone feels their blood boiling.

In the second half, the Seleção got better. Juninho had a few opportunities and managed to escape his markers, but it wasn't to be our day. I can't find any other explanation for what happened. Mexico scored a second goal, and then there was nothing we could do to stage a realistic comeback. The saddest part was to see my son collapsed on the pitch afterwards, covering his face and crying. I, who had seen so many of his joyous moments in other stadiums, collapsed with him right there.

I knew how much he wanted that gold medal, how important that was for him and the new generation, who would go on to represent Brazil at the 2014 World Cup. Unfortunately, our country doesn't tend to recognise the value of third or second place, and more so in football than in other Olympic sports. It's a shame, but that's how it goes: in Brazil, second place is the first loser.

Of course nobody wants to lose. Nevertheless, we need to understand that we never lose on our own. There's always a good opponent on the other side wanting the same things you do. On a number of occasions it's not that we have been the losers as much as our opponents have been the winners. The Mexican players also worked very hard and deserved that victory.

But we needed to shoulder our responsibilities. Juninho was devastated. Afterwards, he spoke to the press and talked about his sadness. It's not easy to speak in a time like that, but I was pleased by the maturity my son was showing.

It was a sad defeat, but how many athletes have an Olympic medal? Looking back, it was a great achievement. With the next World Cup and Olympic Games being hosted by Brazil, can you imagine how big our bet will be then?

In these difficult times, I comfort myself remembering the first months of his life. When he swapped day for night, crying the whole night through. His mother and I, being first-time parents, had no idea what to do, especially me. I was going through a good phase with Mogi Mirim, playing a lot of matches in 1992. In the days before the matches, I couldn't get any rest. It took me a while to learn how to put him to sleep. I used to take off my shirt and put his chest against mine, until he finally nodded off. I think the body warmth calmed him. Those were beautiful moments.

But the next day I always felt very tired, and it was hard to go to work at 10 a.m. to prepare for the matches. That was my profession, the way I provided for my family, and it wasn't easy. My wife tried to take my place to let me sleep more, but I didn't let her. I wanted to be with my son. I was sleeping less, but playing well. Maybe it was my best period as a professional. I think the contact with my son somehow invigorated me. Love is capable of strange things.

I never worried too much about my sleep. I only cared about my son. And I never used him as an excuse when things didn't go well on the pitch. That's why I always tell Neymar Jr never to find excuses for the defeats he suffers. That's what I learned during those first months of his life. I had many excuses to not play well, but I was actually playing better.

So, I say to everyone around me, do your best, and work with enthusiasm, dedication and love. It's that simple.

MATURING

WITH THE BIRTH OF my son in 2011, with everything I had achieved with Santos, with all the support I received from my partners and sponsors, family and friends, and with the enormous affection I felt from the fans, I really didn't need to leave Brazil until 2013.

The happiness I felt was worth everything. I was working with wonderful people, real friends, and everything was great. It didn't feel like the time to leave. But if I did, I had to make that decision myself, together with my family. And no one else.

A lot was said in the media about the direction my career should take. Some opinions were respectable and intelligent. Others were simply unpleasant. There was a period when it seemed like it was the only thing people talked about. If I missed a goal, it was because I wanted to leave Santos. If I scored twice, it was because Brazilian football was too easy and I needed to play overseas. If people tackled me too much, it would be better if I were preserved in Europe. If someone thought I was diving, it was better that I went to Europe, where the referees are stricter. People found motives for me to leave in anything. Even people outside the world of football had something to say. After each match, instead of talking about the victory or the defeat, instead of asking why I played well or badly, the first question always concerned whether I had reached a deal to leave Brazil.

It all began to get on my nerves, but I couldn't say or do anything, because I didn't want to fuel any more gossip. I had to endure the endless speculation and just keep my mouth shut. All I could do was respond on the pitch, by playing well. But to make matters worse, both Santos and I were going through a rough patch at the beginning of 2013. We hadn't qualified for the Libertadores that season, so all we had to play for was the Copa do Brasil, which began later in the year. In the Campeonato Paulista, we had a bad start and it took longer than usual for us to recover, myself included. The great Argentinian Montillo, who had just been hired by Santos, had very little time to adapt to our team and we struggled in the Campeonato Paulista.

Nevertheless, we carried on and made it to the quarter-final, where we beat Palmeiras in a penalty shootout at Vila Belmiro. In the semi-final, against Mogi Mirim, we also beat their great team in a penalty shootout. I cried a lot at the end of that tough match. I felt a great relief and joy for making it through to the final. And all the press had a field day speculating as to why I was so emotional.

In the final against Corinthians, we faced another stern battle. They won the first match, at the Pacaembu Stadium, 2-1. In the second match, at Vila Belmiro, we scored first, but they managed to tie the match and hold on until the end. We missed, at home, the chance to do something that even Pelé hadn't: win the Campeonato Paulista four times in a row. No team has ever done that.

We gave it our best shot, but it wasn't enough. It was the fifth consecutive time that Santos had made the final of that competition, and between 2006 and 2013 the only year we didn't was in 2008. That's remarkable. Still, there was a great deal of pressure on us, as if everything we had achieved previously didn't matter. Amid this great maelstrom of pressure, expectation and constant speculation, I finally decided that it really was time for a change. The time had come to take on other challenges.

BARCELONA

BARCELONA HAD FLIRTED WITH us since 2011, but there had never been a serious proposal. A lot was said in the Brazilian and Spanish press, with some people claiming to know all the details of the alleged deal. That's normal in any negotiation. What was not normal was the number of people trying to force the situation, often giving malicious and false details in the press.

They said many things without a single shred of proof about what was actually happening. Everything that Neymar Jr and I said at the time proved to be true later on. There was never an auction for his rights, and we hadn't made any previous deal. We didn't hurt Santos, or anyone else, financially.

We just thought it was time to go. We weren't closing a door forever, because you don't do that to your own home, to a club that is so close to your heart. However, it was time for Neymar Jr and our family to look for new horizons. It was the right time in all aspects: emotionally, professionally, financially, and above all, personally. It was time to take a step further, to grow and to develop. That's the path of any professional in any career.

It's absurd when someone says that an athlete is a 'mercenary' when he changes clubs. What about any person who trades one company for another after receiving a better offer? Is this person also a mercenary? Of course not. But in football, the passion makes people think in odd ways.

The negotiation was good for everyone. Considering the circumstances, the parts involved, and the various interests, we did well. We did the right thing, at the right moment, and with the right club. Santos always supported us, and we always believed in them, including former president Marcelo Teixeira and the current president Luis Álvaro. We always had the support and understanding of everyone. We never governed the direction of Juninho's career based on financial gain; we always concentrated first and foremost on his happiness. Few players in recent times have stayed so long in one club in Brazilian football. He stayed at Santos for all those years, turning down other offers, because that's what he wanted. And it was also what Santos wanted. A series of partners and sponsors made that happen, ever since he was first signed in 2006, when the club saw the potential of a 13-year-old kid. And we will always be thankful for that. Neymar Jr left Santos, but Santos will never leave his heart, just as it has always been with me and with Juninho's grandfather.

It was important that he went to a club like Barcelona with a great structure and an incredible team. Juninho was eager to blend in as fast as he could. Seeing him play alongside players like Messi and in a stadium like Camp Nou has been incredible. Messi is an exemplary person and athlete. For me, a football aficionado, seeing my son playing alongside the best player in the world gives me the same joy that I'm sure Neymar Jr feels doing it.

It's a great group to work with, and they all welcomed Juninho with open arms. Messi himself insisted on speaking with Neymar Jr right after word came out that the deal was done. He said that everyone was happy for him, and they were all waiting eagerly for his arrival. And so it proved.

I'm really happy that Juninho has good relations with everyone in the football world. When David Beckham was on loan at Paris Saint-Germain, Leonardo, a World Cup winner with Brazil in 1994 and former manager at the French club, contacted Neymar Jr on behalf of Beckham. His oldest son, Brooklyn, despite being a Real Madrid supporter, is also a great fan of Juninho's. Beckham asked for an autographed jersey for his son. Soon after, he called Neymar Jr himself to thank him for the present. To be able to mix so freely with the best players in the world like that really is amazing and shows the regard in which he is held.

But to me, he will always be my little boy. I'll always remember riding the bus with him, taking him to training on my motorcycle, traveling endlessly to give him every opportunity that I could and to try to fulfil all his dreams. Barcelona is the next step on that journey.

MI CASA, SU CASA

C AN YOU IMAGINE WHAT it's like for a boy who used to play in the streets and at the beach to arrive in a strange city aged just 21 and be introduced to a stadium packed with 56,000 people? It was amazing and wonderful!

I was with the Seleção preparing to play in the Confederations Cup. I played on a Sunday for Brazil, then I travelled to Barcelona and then, the following Monday, I was introduced at Camp Nou.

I could barely contain my emotions. It was a dream come true. When I played video games, I always made my character play for the greatest clubs in the world. Now, I was going to do it for real. I was going to play alongside the incomparable Messi and with all the other incredible footballers at the club, who had established themselves as the greatest team in the world, one that many believe to be the greatest team ever.

The thrill of entering Camp Nou and receiving a standing ovation from all those fans was just incredible. I can't explain how it felt. That's what I said in the press conference afterwards, when I couldn't hold back my tears any longer.

Before the interview, they showed a video of my goals for Santos and Brazil. Of course, they showed the goal against Flamengo, which won the Puskás Award, and the goal against Internacional in the 2012 Libertadores, which was also nominated for the goal of the year.

I already knew that I had made the right choice, at the right time and with the right club when I switched from Santos to Barcelona, but if I had any lingering doubts, they dissolved right then and there. And I thought it was funny when they showed images of my father during the presentation, always with a dead serious face, looking like a coach a few minutes before the end of a tough match. But even just wearing that famous blue and red jersey for a few minutes overwhelmed me. My family and friends were all emotional, and I looked across at my father, who was trying his best to hold it all in, but I could see how proud he was of me. That face was the proof that we made all the right choices. We built a great history with Santos that none of us will ever forget. With Brazil, there's still a whole career ahead of me. And now, with Barcelona, I feel I have so much to achieve.

Now, it's time for me to do my part and help my teammates to win every tournament we play. This is not a promise, but it's a wish – a wish that could come true with a club like Barcelona, with its players and structure. The group is so amazing that if you'd let me, I'd spend this whole book talking about them.

The jersey is different to one I grew up wanting to play in, but I play with the same dedication and passion for Barcelona that I felt when I played for Santos. And while the club and the jersey may have changed, some things stay the same. On the bus rides to the stadiums, or even in the dressing rooms, I always call my father before I play. We talk about the match, the opponent, our team, we talk about the things I could do and the things I shouldn't do. We chat about football, family and life. And then we say a short prayer, always ending with Isaiah: 'No weapon formed against you shall prosper, and every tongue which rises against you in judgment, you shall condemn. This is the heritage of the servants of the Lord, and their righteousness is from Me, says the Lord.'

Then I am ready.

2013 CONFEDERATIONS CUP

BEFORE THE SECOND MATCH of the competition, against Mexico, my son made a statement about the protests that were taking place in Brazil at the time. Neymar Jr wrote the following on his Facebook page:

> I'm sad about everything that's happening in Brazil. I always had faith that we would never come to the point where we needed to 'take to the streets' to demand better transport, health, education and security, because I always felt that those were OBLIGATIONS of our government . . . My parents worked hard to give me and my sister a minimum quality of life . . . Today, thanks to the success you allowed me to have, supporting the cause of the protests all over our country could seem inflammatory on my part, but it's not: I'm BRAZILIAN and I love my country! My family and friends live in Brazil! That's

why I also want a more just country, with more security, a better health system, and more HONESTY!!! The only way that I have to represent and defend Brazil is by playing football... And from this match onwards I'll be inspired by these protests... #TamoJunto

I was very pleased with my son's statement and that he wasn't afraid of the potential repercussions. He cannot fear becoming alienated, and he can't abstain from saying his opinions. Because of his position in the Seleção and in society, it's also his duty to speak his mind, to open his heart and show his feelings. He may live in the world of football, but that doesn't mean he can hide from the real world.

On the pitch, we had a good start in the Confederations Cup, and Neymar Jr played fantastically. He scored a beautiful goal against Japan with his first touch. That goal gave a confidence to the team that allowed them to do what they do best. Japan had a good team, but the Seleção played better. At the beginning of the second half, Paulinho scored again, and in the last minute, Jô made it 3-0. They played well and deserved the victory. The fans were also amazing, supporting the team through every minute of the match.

The match against Mexico was also amazing. The fans in Fortaleza sung the national anthem with incredible passion before kick-off and it was clear to see how that inspired the players. Neymar Jr was again fortunate enough to score right at the beginning, this time with his left foot. It was his best game in the competition, maybe his best for Brazil, at least at that time. In the second half, he made another sensational play and passed to Jô, who scored our second goal. Neymar Jr was awarded Man of the Match by FIFA. He deserved it. After five matches with Brazil, he had won the award four times. Those four trophies are now on display in pride of place at our office in Santos.

Now, it was time for Italy, a great rival who had almost bested us in a 2-2 draw earlier in the year. This time, however, urged on by another magnificent crowd, the Seleção played very well and stormed to victory. Dante opened the scoring just before half-time, before Italy equalised shortly after the break. Soon after, my son was knocked down on the edge of the area. As the referee blew his whistle, Juninho picked himself up and prepared himself for the resulting shot at goal. He saw the goalkeeper edging towards the right, and whipped the ball to the opposite side to make it 2-1.

Fred scored again after a great long pass from Marcelo. Then, Italy scored a goal after a confusing passage of play: the referee called a penalty, but then backtracked. I had never seen anything like that before. But afterwards, even with all the pressure from Italy, Marcelo and Fred once again took matters into their own hands, and Fred made the final score 4-2.

With three victories in the group phase, our confidence was high. However, our opponent in the semi-final was Uruguay, another great historical derby. Lugano, the Uruguayan defender, said before the match that Neymar Jr had a habit of diving and that Brazilian football wasn't what it used to be. Nothing that we hadn't heard before.

With football, all that matters is what happens on the pitch. The first half was very tough. The fans were again amazing during the national anthem and kept up the energy and the noise throughout the match. Uruguay played very well, even better than us at times. But the Seleção responded to the support from the crowd. In the final minutes of the first half, Paulinho sent a majestic long pass from the midfield; Juninho controlled it with his chest, brought the ball down and fired a shot at the keeper, who just managed to parry the ball away, but Fred caught the rebound and scored.

Right after the restart, just as Italy had done, Uruguay scored an equaliser. The match was again tough for us, and continued that way until the end. In many ways it felt like the players were fighting more than playing. At a corner kick, one of their players said some things to my son, trying to aggravate him. But Juninho played along, blew him some kisses and kept his cool. The TV replayed those kisses again and again. It was funny.

And it was from a corner kick that we scored the winning goal. Neymar Jr fired the ball into the ten yard box, right on Paulinho's head, who expertly directed it home to make it 2-1 with only five minutes left. Soon after, coach Luiz Felipe Scolari, who had returned to his position with the Seleção in November 2012, replaced Juninho and he left the field to rapturous applause. The team had qualified for the final, which was to be played at the Maracaná Stadium in Rio against the opponent that everybody wanted: Spain. The world champions, two-time European champions and a team full of Juninho's Barcelona teammates: Iniesta, Xavi, Busquets, Pedro, Piqué, Villa, Valdés, Jordi, Alba, and Fábreagas.

For all these glorious achievements, Spain had yet to prove they were the best team at the 2013 Confederations Cup. And the only way to do that was to beat Brazil, the five-time World Cup champions and three-time Confederations Cup champions, playing at home. It was a clash between giants.

One of the major Achilles heels of Brazilian football is the lack of playing time that the Seleção players have together. But as the tournament went on, the better they became, the more comfortable they were with each other and the better the spirit was in the squad.

In the final against Spain, the team seemed to become even stronger after the stadium boomed out the Brazilian national anthem. That's when we started to win the match. And sure enough, after a little more than a minute, Fred scored our first goal. Hulk crossed the ball from the right, Neymar Jr didn't control it well, but Fred, despite being on the ground (I had never seen anything like it), fired the ball into the net.

And we almost scored again six minutes later, through Oscar, and this effort was followed up by Paulinho, who almost scored with a long ball over their goalie. Of course, Iker Casillas is not just any goalkeeper, and he scrambled back to save. But Brazil played just like in the glory days: we smothered their team, never giving them an inch of space to play. When their striker Pedro escaped our defence, our defender David Luiz saved the ball on the goal line. The entire stadium celebrated like we had scored.

You can imagine how it was when Neymar Jr scored the second goal, with less than three minutes to go in the first half. He traded quick passes with Oscar and struck with his left foot. It was a superb goal. At half-time the boys were exultant, and came back with the same concentration as before. Hulk epitomised the spirit and the intentions of the team when he scored to make it 3-0.

Shortly afterwards, Spain had a penalty kick that Sergio Ramos missed. With 22 minutes gone in the second half, Piqué tripped Neymar Jr and was shown a red card. With the one-man advantage the Seleção pressed forward, but they missed a lot of opportunities. Still, 3-0 was beyond our wildest expectations.

When the match was over, Juninho hugged the first Spaniard he saw. Then, he complimented all the referees and was the first to shake hands with our great opponents, many of whom were to become his teammates. After that, he went to the fans to thank them for their support. If he could, he would have hugged the entire stadium. In the press conference, he insisted on wearing the jersey of his teammate, Leandro Damião, who had suffered an injury before the tournament and missed the competition. Leandro was as much a champion as everyone else.

That's how you build a group and a winning team. Ever since he played futsal as a child, Juninho has learned that you need to work within the group. It's the old story of all for one and one for all. That's also how we run our company: we all work for Neymar Jr, and he works for us.

Soon afterwards, there was another thrill for him and, of course, for me: he received the Bronze Boot award as the third-highest scorer of the competition. Fernando Torres and Fred each scored five times, Neymar Jr scored four times. This trophy is also in my office. Afterwards, he was awarded the greatest honour a player can receive: the Golden Ball, given to the best player in the competition. He never thought he would win a title like that ahead of Iniesta, in second place, and Paulinho in third. And this was in a competition that also featured players like Pirlo and Cavani. It was an honour and a privilege.

At 9.13 p.m., in the middle of the Maracaná Stadium, Juninho lifted his second trophy of the night, pointing to the skies and thanking God for another achievement. Soon after, when he received the gold medal, he also received kisses from the presidents of FIFA and the Brazilian Football Confederation. Up there on the stage, he waited for our captain to lift the most important award of the night: the 2013 Confederations Cup. The stadium erupted with the cries of 'Campeão!' Brazil were the champions!

Neymar Jr joined his teammates to pose with the trophy for the photographers before embarking on a lap of honour around the stadium. Later, he posed for a photo with all his trophies, like he was just a fan. And indeed he is: he's a fan that had the privilege to play for his national team. Once more, thanks to God, he played like a classic Brazilian player. As a father, I know I'm biased, but as a football aficionado, I'm also really happy with what Juninho and his teammates did for Brazilian football. We found our lost pride with that victory. We were champions again, putting on a great show for the fans, playing with intelligence, skill and speed.

We won as a truly Brazilian team, in our own home, with five victories in five matches and a 3-0 score against the world champions. I guess that says it all.

DAVI LUCCA

WHEN I WAS TOLD I was going to be a father, at 19, just before the final match of the 2011 Campeonato Paulista, I confess I didn't know how to react. It was a difficult time, with so much going on around me. I was afraid of all the responsibilities. I felt I wasn't ready yet. It was too soon. I cried a lot at first.

Telling my family wasn't easy either. So I built up the courage and went to speak with my mother. I asked her to stay at home so we could talk. When I told her, she became very emotional and started to cry. Telling the new grandfather wasn't so easy. I couldn't find the words at first. My father has always given me advice, about everything, telling me about the consequences of everything I do.

However, after the initial shock, my father embraced the situation with open arms and went with me to talk to Carol, the mother of my son. He was incredible, as always. Her family were also very supportive and everything has been great since then, we all get along very well.

My father helped me a lot. The minute he knew he was going to be a grandfather he gave me all the support that I needed. He told me that the love he feels for me and my sister is infinite. And even if I didn't marry or stay with Carol, Davi would always be part of our family.

A son is a blessing. That's what Davi Lucca will always be. He is a blessing in the lives of his parents, his grandparents, his aunts and uncles, of all his family. My life became so much more special after his arrival. Today and every day, Davi is my joy and my happiness. I'm an enthusiastic father. I love to play and be around him. I love to see him grow. I teach and I learn from him. I'd do anything for him. I even change his nappies. I try to do with my son everything my father did with me. It's a delight, especially because I have a great relationship with his mother. We talk a lot, because I want to participate as much as I can in his education. I want him to be a good human being, so I'll educate him the best way I can, just like my parents did with me. I do everything with him, and for him.

The first time I took him to a stadium was in a derby against Corinthians at Vila Belmiro. It was 4 March 2012. He was only six months old, but I didn't care: I assumed the responsibility. My friends got me a tiny Santos jersey and a little hat. I walked onto the pitch holding him in my arms. There was a big uproar. Almost nobody knew I would do that. Not even his grandfather. I asked Carol and she was okay with it. It was such a joy to hold him on that sunny Sunday. His godfather, Ganso, gave him a kiss before I gave him back to his mother. And, of course, he was a lucky charm: we won 1-0!

Davi Lucca will be the same thing I was to my father: the mascot of my teams. There's a picture of my father playing for Juiz de Fora, in 1994. The team is posing for the traditional picture, and in the middle of all those big guys, you can see a tiny kid in front of my father. That's me! On that day in Vila Belmiro, Davi Lucca was the only thing to me in the entire stadium.

He was born at 11 a.m. on 24 August 2011 – I don't care much for numbers, but it's interesting that in 2011, at 11 in the morning, the son of the player who wore the number 11 jersey for Santos was born, whose father was champion of 2011 Campeonato Paulista and Libertadores, and more than that – a champion for having Davi Lucca.

Since that day, I don't think about myself anymore. I think about him: my son. I understand my father a lot more with each day that passes. There's no feeling like fatherhood. It's a joy that thrills and blesses me. I hope Davi Lucca will have idols and role models like I had. I just hope I don't end up in the same situation as Robinho: when we played together in Santos, he used to take his son to the training sessions, and the kid would say that he was *my* fan.

I'm already preparing myself for that, because Davi probably won't say that he is a fan of Neymar Jr. But I have no problems in admitting that I am a proud fan of Davi Lucca. Now, I'm focused on playing and scoring for him. My son is my one true love in life.

PRIDE

ARLY ON, I HAD one objective: to take care of Juninho until his debut as a professional footballer. I would only feel fulfilled when I saw him taking to the pitch for the first time in a major competition. I guess I did my part. Now it's up to him. Of course, he'll always have the support of his family right behind him. Since his debut in 2009, we have done everything for him, because we are truly a team.

Now, will he become the best in the world? We hear that question a lot. Honestly, that's not our ambition. That's not why Juninho plays. If someday FIFA awards him as the best player in a season, it will be the result of a job well done. If we wanted him to be the best in the world, we would have complied with what people told us: 'To be the best, you have to play against the best. If you go to Barcelona, you will always be in Messi's shadow.'

Many people have yet to understand how we work with Juninho. Neymar Jr only wants to be happy. He's been that way since he was born, and since he started to play football. He wants to play among the best and he chose what he likes best: the beautiful football of Barcelona. That's good for him and for those who love the sport.

Just like Xavi said, 'I don't play to be the best in the world. I help my teammates to be the best in the world.' That's it. Football is a collective sport. Neymar Jr is very happy at Barcelona and he just wants to make people happy with his football.

When we see the likes of Tostão, the great Brazilian footballer, saying good things about him it is very reassuring. I'll never forget a TV advert Volkswagen made which featured Ayrton Senna and the Dalai Lama, among other important figures, alongside my son. It's not vanity, it is pure pride. And respect for his skills. I watched that ad a million times. Because I know how much we worked to have that kind of recognition.

What I wanted most in my life was to hear people saying good things about my children. In that regard, I'm also very blessed. People like what Juninho does with the ball and also in life. My son suffered from prejudice first-hand playing with the Seleção. He heard all kinds of things shouted from the stadium seats. At times, he lost it. He's not a machine, and sometimes people demand too much from him. Good thing I'm seasoned; the life I had was really tough. There were often times when I couldn't buy presents for him and Rafaela. But I always said that someday things were going to be different. I allowed Neymar to dream big. The only thing I could always give to my children was the incentive to dream. And so they did.

What really impresses me with Juninho is his ability to read the match, from his perspective and from the opponent's perspective. Many footballers just play the match, they don't read it. Neymar Jr can play and also see the movements of his team and the opposition. Sometimes it seems like he's watching the match from the stadium seats instead of being on the pitch.

He has an amazing ability to absorb and learn. When he shoots something for TV, he always learns his lines in a second. He can remember every detail of his many matches. A lot of people in football can barely remember what they did or didn't do on the pitch, but not Juninho. He always reviews everything he did and is always trying to learn from it.

Another very important thing in his career has been his patience to mature. I know he was a precocious child, doing things sooner in football than his peers, but he didn't rush his development as an athlete or as a person. He always understood that you can't skip some stages in life. His body, at 17, was the body of a 17-year-old kid. At 19, it was the body of a 19-year-old athlete, and so on. He will succeed in life because he knows that there's a right time for everything. I may point the way, but he is the one who decides for himself. He almost always chooses right. So it's important to remember that regardless of what path he chose before, it was always his decision. Although we take care of many things for him so he can concentrate on his football, he ultimately makes all the big decisions about his life and career. And that's how it should be.

Every match matters for him. And we both think that the titles are a consequence of hard work. After the opening match of the under-20 South American competition in Peru, when Brazil won 4-2 against Paraguay, even the Argentinean press recognised his talents. *Olé* newspaper ran a front-cover headline that read 'Neymaradona' after he scored all four of Brazil's goals. You can image what a thrill it was for me. To this day Pelé and Maradona are compared to each other, but to see the Argentineans themselves comparing Maradona to my son was just incredible.

I want to watch every time he plays, not just because he's my son, but because it is a pleasure to watch a footballer playing with such love and dedication. Sometimes, I wince when I see some of the hard tackles he takes. But there are funny moments. Once, Brazil were playing against Argentina and, as is always the case between the two, the match was very tough. At some point, Neymar started to dribble past everyone, until he was pulled back by the defender, Guiñazu. The referee called the foul, but the Argentinean player complained that he had done nothing wrong while trying to let go of something in his hand: he had ripped a number off Juninho's shirt!

So, for the rest of the match, Juninho was player with a number one on his back instead of 11. Well, for me, he is always number one.

It was one of those moments that you never forget. I'm sure we'll have many more joys. After all, Juninho is still only in the early years of his career. There's still a lot to come for him. With his commitment and love for what he does, with the affection of those who support him, and with the structure of his teams, I know he will achieve much more.

I hope that at the end of his career, my son receives recognition not only for his talent, but also for the humble way he has treated everyone. I hope to hear from the people who have known him since he was a tiny, skinny kid running after the ball, that after he grew up he kept treating people with the same respect and affection as he did back then. Everything he receives from his fans, he tries to give back. Not just because that's how he was raised by Nadine and me, but because that's who he is.

My son is a nice guy. He's a decent person. That's all that matters in life: to be a good person. I can say that not just because I'm his father, but because I've know him since his birth. And I do demand a lot from him, and also from myself. It's not easy to be a father and a fan at the same time. I try, as much as possible, not to mix these two things up. I try to be the father first, and then I allow myself to be a fan. But, again, it's not easy.

I know Davi Lucca will be very proud of his father. I know many kids will feel the joy of watching Neymar Jr and his teammates. I know he'll live to see and do a lot of great things.

My son is my treasure. And a treasure for all fans of Santos, Barcelona and Brazil.

THE FUTURE

WHAT WILL BE MY future? Where will I be ten years from now? I don't know. I hope I can continue to do what makes me happy. I hope I can still bring joy to the fans of Santos, Barcelona, Brazil, and everyone else who loves football.

I want to bring joy to the fans of the sport. I don't train to be the best in the world. I don't play to show off. I play to help my club and my teammates. I play for my country. I play because I love football.

In the past few years I have had to grow up a lot. Things happened very fast; I started playing for the Santos professional team at 17 and became a father at 19. All that gave me a lot of experience that I wouldn't have otherwise. I feel comfortable playing any match, in any stadium, in any country. I have learned from everything that has happened to me, and also because I have the best guide and teacher in the world: my father. If ever

I was sad for any reason, he would tell me, 'You'll learn from it all, son. You may cry now, but later you'll look back and you will realise that it all made you grow.'

I'll do all I can to keep getting better. Hopefully, I'll become world champion in 2014, in my own country. Who knows, maybe even win again in 2018? I'll do my best to bring the happiness that our people deserve.

I know I'll always receive encouragement from my father for everything. He stands by my side today, and will continue fighting for me and my family in the future. I only got where I am because I had my father to orientate and support me. He is primarily responsible for me being where I am. He suffered a lot, and he does everything he can so I don't go through the same things he did. I can't predict the future, but I know my family will always be there.

I thank God for the affection I received from all Santos' fans, from 2009 to 2013, and I am so thankful for the enthusiastic welcome I now receive from the fans at Barcelona, and I am thankful for the love I receive from Brazil's fans. They will always be with me. I can't promise goals, victories, and titles, because it doesn't depend only on me. But I can promise to fight with all I've got. Football is not only about victory, draw, or defeat. It's much more than that. It's not just *we* versus *them*. Football is a child's game that grown-ups take seriously. But it doesn't need to be serious all the time. I want to have fun. I want to make people happy. I want to keep running, playing, dribbling and scoring. I always wanted to be a footballer. When I used to watch my father playing, I fantasised about doing the same. If a child has a dream, he must chase it. And never give up, even if people say it will never come true. I want to be the boy who never stopped dreaming.

I believed in my dream. Deep down, I am still that little kid who used to run up and down the seats in the stadium. I want to always be the little kid that played association football in the morning, studied in the afternoon, played futsal in the evening, and finally went home late at night riding with his father in the family's old car.

Dad, you are my hero, my adviser, my friend. There are not enough words to thank you for so much love and dedication. For you and for my mum, the woman of my life, I would do anything. I thank God for having the two of you by my side. I want to be to Davi Lucca everything that you are to me. And that is why I wanted us to write this book together, because this is our story, not just mine. I hope I get to write more victorious chapters in this life, with victories that aren't made just with results, but with the love of playing, with the joy of being the son of Neymar, and with the happiness of being Neymar Jr.

EPILOGUE

THREE MINUTES. THAT – AND a thunderous strike, of course – was all Neymar Jr needed to silence his critics. As he slammed home the opening goal of the Seleção's 2013 Confederations Cup campaign at the Mané Garrincha National Stadium in Brasília, the 60,000-plus crowd erupted. All the doubters who had been hounding him were stunned into silence. When Neymar's less-favoured left boot sent the ball flying past the Japanese goalkeeper it put an end to a nine-game dry spell that critics had been using as exhibit A to prove their theory that the striker's shoulders weren't broad enough to support the weight of Brazil's expectation. In previous Seleção games he had been booed and after a friendly against Chile in April 2013, certain sections of the Brazilian support had labelled him a bottler. Throw into the mix his recently announced move from Santos FC to Barcelona and one can begin to get a sense of the pressure that Neymar Jr was under going into the Confederations Cup.

That strike was followed by another three goals in the competition, including another wonderful left-footed howitzer against the mighty Spain in a 3-0 drubbing, during which Neymar tormented several future Barcelona teammates and got Gerard Piqué sent off after the defender upended him in a desperate attempt to stop another counterattack. Neymar's smile when celebrating on the Maracaná pitch at full time showed his unadulterated joy and sense of achievement in the team's success.

He would finish the pre-World Cup cycle in March 2014 by scoring his 30th goal in 47 games for the Seleção. Neymar Jr reached that milestone in fewer games than Cristiano Ronaldo and Lionel Messi took to score 30 for Portugal and Argentina respectively. Following on from Ronaldinho Gaúcho and Kaka, Neymar became the new icon for the Seleção, whether he wanted to be thought of in that way or not.

Even though he hadn't been on the plane that took Brazil to the 2010 World Cup, Neymar had been a recurrent topic with fans both anonymous and famous (the late great Sócrates, for example), many of whom had demanded that manager Dunga took him to South Africa. As we all know now, the Seleção crashed out of that tournament in the quarter-finals and new manager Mano Menezes didn't bat an eyelid before calling up Neymar for his Seleção debut in a friendly against the United States in August 2010. The striker duly repaid Menezes' faith by scoring one of the Seleção's goals in a 2-0 victory. A year later, Neymar Jr was instrumental in Santos FC's victory in the Copa Libertadores da América (the South American version of the UEFA Champions League), a trophy that the club had last won in the 1960s, when Pelé was still playing.

His success has not gone unnoticed by prospective sponsors. Neymar is almost omnipresent in adverts in the Brazilian media. That he has amongst his advisors the same Simon Oliveira who used to advise David Beckham speaks volumes about his marketability. Sports marketing experts have no doubts that his commercial potential already challenges Messi's, even though, on the pitch, Neymar Jr himself is in no rush to upstage his four-time Ballon d'Or winning club-mate.

Throughout all these mesmerising highs, Neymar Sr has remained a crucial influence, a buffer against the understandable frenzy that his son's life has become. In him, Juninho has a rock, a friend, and a role model. He wants his son to touch the stars and to realise the dreams he has had since he was a child, but he will never allow Neymar Jr's feet to leave the ground. Football could do more with cases like that.

Fernando Duarte, London, May 2014

AWARDS

Champion of the 2013 FIFA Confederations Cup

Golden Ball – Player of the 2013 FIFA Confederations Cup

Bronze Boot – Third highest scorer of 2013 FIFA Confederations Cup with 4 goals

Player of the 2013 Campeonato Paulista

Second highest scorer of the 2013 Campeonato Paulista with 12 goals

2012 South American Footballer of the Year – *El País*

2012 South America Dream Team – *El País*

Troféu Mesa Redonda – Player of the 2012 Campeonato Brasileiro

Troféu Mesa Redonda – Best forward of the 2012 Campeonato Brasileiro

Troféu Armando Nogueira 2012 – SporTV and GloboEsporte.com

Prêmio Globolinha de Ouro – Best goal of the 2012 Campeonato Brasileiro

Golden Ball *Hors-Concours* – *Placar* and ESPN Brasil

Golden Boot – *Placar* and ESPN Brasil

2012 Campeonato Brasileiro Dream Team

Prêmio Brasil Olímpico 2012 – Brazilian Olympic Committee

Champion of the 2012 Recopa Sudamericana

Player of the 2012 Recopa Sudamericana

Silver Medal – 2012 Summer Olympic Games

Top Striker of the 2012 Libertadores da América with 8 goals

Libertadores da América Dream Team

Champion of the 2012 Campeonato Paulista

Top Striker of the 2012 Campeonato Paulista with 20 goals

Player of the 2012 Campeonato Paulista

2012 Campeonato Paulista Dream Team

FIFA Puskás Award – Best goal of 2011

2011 South American Footballer of the Year – *El País*

Bronze Ball – Third best player of 2013 FIFA Club World Cup

Golden Ball – Player of the 2011 Campeonato Brasileiro (*Placar* and ESPN Brasil)

Silver Ball – 2011 Campeonato Brasileiro Dream Team (*Placar* and ESPN Brasil)

Golden Boot 2011 – *Placar* and ESPN Brasil

Troféu Armando Nogueira 2011 – SporTV and GloboEsporte.com

Prêmio Brasil Olímpico 2011 – Brazilian Olympic Committee

Player of the 2011 Campeonato Brasileiro

2011 Campeonato Brasileiro Dream Team

Player of the 2011 Libertadores da América

Prêmio Ginga Esporte Interativo – Best goal of 2011

Prêmio Ginga Esporte Interativo – Player of the 2011 season

Second highest scorer of the 2011 Libertadores da América with 6 goals

Champion of the 2011 Libertadores da América

Player of the 2011 Campeonato Paulista

2011 Campeonato Paulista Dream Team

Champion of the 2011 Campeonato Paulista

Top Striker at the 2011 South American Youth Championship with 9 goals

Champion of the 2011 South American Youth Championship

Top Striker at the 2010 Copa do Brasil with 11 goals

Champion of the 2010 Copa do Brasil

2010 Campeonato Paulista Dream Team

Player of the 2010 Campeonato Paulista

Champion of the 2010 Campeonato Paulista

Best young player of the 2009 Campeonato Paulista

INSTITUTO PROJETO NEYMAR JR

IN THE CITY OF Praia Grande, in the region of Jardim Glória, the same place where Neymar Sr built his little house many years ago, a dream is coming true. However, this is not the dream of one family: it's a dream for everyone who lives in the region, who will have a centre that promotes life, health, sport and education.

The Instituto Projeto Neymar Jr is a private non-profit association dedicated to social causes. It is building a complex for sports and educational purposes, which intends to serve families with low income. The mission of the institute is to contribute to the social and educational growth of the families, promoting physical activity and providing access to culture for thousands of people.

Through sport, the institute's objective is to expand the horizons of the children, the families and all of the community, transmitting specific knowledge and information that enriches the lives of the citizens so they can grow in a better environment.

The complex has 8,400 square meters of land and will initially have 2,300 children attending from the ages of 7 to 14. Their parents will also attend, totalling more than ten thousand people. The parents will have access to lectures (on home economics, health, motivation, etc.), courses on professional development, recycling, and adult literacy, among others.

All the activities will be held at the complex, which is situated in an area given by the city of Praia Grande in a system of concession for the first 30 years, with the option to extend for 30 more years. The site lies in Jardim Glória, and will accessible to those from the microregions of Aeroclube, Aprazível, Guaramar, Guilermima, Marília, São Sebastião, Sítio do Campo, and Vila Sônia.

The criteria for the use of the place by the children and their families was established as follows: they must reside in the region, they must attend the municipal schools of José Júlio, Roberto Santini, Elza Oliveira, or Maria Nilza, with an attendance of at least 90%, and their parents must participate in the activities.

The institute is designed to offer new opportunities to the community that Neymar Jr grew up in. He is helping to write new history both on and off the pitch.

The institute will be built with its own funds and private sponsorship. The activities will use resources from individuals, legal entities and also spontaneous donations to give the community what Neymar Jr didn't have while he was growing up. The inspiration to make this dream come true came from his tough childhood. In his own words, 'When I was a kid, all I wanted was a place like this to go, but there was nothing like it anywhere near.' His father also explains, 'We don't want to wait till Neymar Jr retires to start the project. It's important to build it while he still plays. We'll bring education to the entire family, so the parents can help their children to make the right choices. The family must grow and stay together.'

Nadine hopes to transform the reality that she experienced with her husband. 'We know the real necessities of the region. We can make it better.' Rafaela has the same conviction as her mother. 'The institute is a dream of our family. We'll make it come true to improve the life of many people in the community.'